Pennine Way

Da
out
ma
not
He
An
Ne
had
pos
lov
regularly to *Country Walking* and
Outdoor Fitness, and lives in the
south Cotswolds with his wife
daughter and an irrational
of reservoirs. www.damian

Pennine Way

Damian Hall

Aurum
in association with

NATURAL
ENGLAND

Acknowledgements

A huge thank you to Steve Westwood, the Trail Officer, for his vast knowledge; to Graham Coster, for a wonderful opportunity and a leap of faith; to Jonathan Manning, for mentoring and mentioning my name; to Tony Hopkins, for the excellent guides that preceded this one; to Brenda and Robert Updegraff for their caring work; to Mark Bauer, for photography tuition; to Kelvin and Barbara, for taking me outdoors; to Amy, for letting me go bog-trotting when I should have been nappy-changing; to Indigo – sorry for skipping nappy duty, I hope I make you proud in other ways; to walkers I met along the way; and most of all, to Tom Stephenson – what a good idea that was.

Cover photograph: *View from Whitelaw Nick, The Cheviots*
Half-title page: *High Cup*
Title page: *Looking back at Thwaite from halfway up Kisdon Hill*

Aurum Press want to ensure that these National Trail Guides are always as up to date as possible – but stiles collapse, pubs close and bus services change all the time. If, on walking this path, you discover any important changes of which future walkers need to be aware, do let us know. Either email us on **trailguides@aurumpress.co.uk** with your comments, or if you take the trouble to drop us a line to:

Trail Guides, Aurum Press, 7 Greenland Street, London NW1 0ND,
we'll send you a free guide of your choice as thanks.

Contents

How to use this guide

This guide to the Pennine Way is in four parts.

Introduction

An introduction to the Pennine Way, Britain's oldest and toughest National Trail. All your initial questions answered, starting with the most important one: why walk it? Plus, the walk's history (including Alfred Wainwright and the Way), its world-renowned flora and feral fauna, its epic landscapes and intriguing geology.

There is practical advice, such as guidance on when to walk the Pennine Way, how long it might take, what it might cost, an overview of accommodation, transport, signposting and navigation, preparation, equipment, sustainable walking and conservation, safety and potential hazards. There's also information on walking with dogs and the Way's best bits (for those who don't have time to walk it all in one go, quite yet).

Route description

The route is split into 16 days, each with a detailed route description, especially around spots most likely to cause topographical embarrassment, and including GPS references. At the start of each section there are daily stats (distance in miles and kilometres, total ascent and descent for the day, lowest and highest points in feet and metres) and plenty of information on highlights, local history, fauna and flora you may see as you walk. 'Things to look out for' are described at the start of each section and highlighted in bold **blue** type at the appropriate point of the route description; other points of interest are given a reference number that appears in the route description and on the map. To help you keep to the right route, important landmarks and points to look out for along the way are indicated by letters in the route description and on the maps. A black arrow (➜) at the edge of a map indicates the direction of travel. At the end of each section you'll find practical information on transport, accommodation, refreshments, food shops, toilets, cafés and pubs, as well as alternative stop-off suggestions. There's also plenty of Alfred Wainwright whingeing about it all.

Useful information

An archive of contacts for planning the walk, especially transport, accommodation, and baggage-courier services, and a bibliography to get your bright orange whistles whetted. Throughout the book, **green** text indicates that contact details are shown under 'Useful Information'.

Key maps index

Key map 5

Key map 4

Key map 3

Key map 2

Key map 1

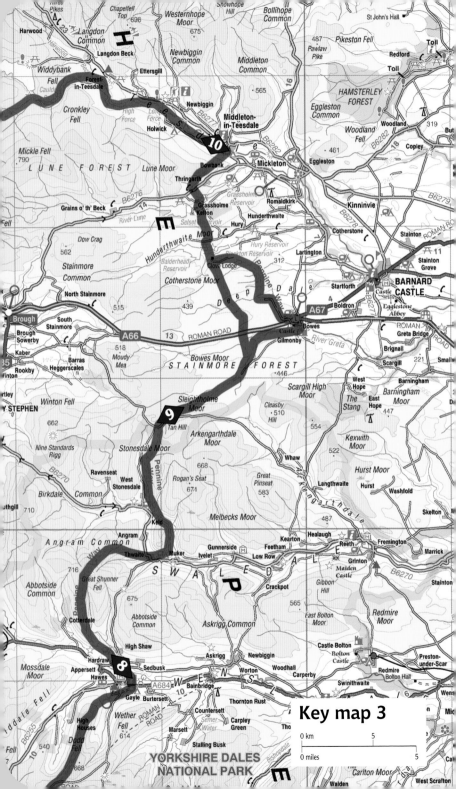

Key map 3

0 km ———— 5

0 miles ———— 5

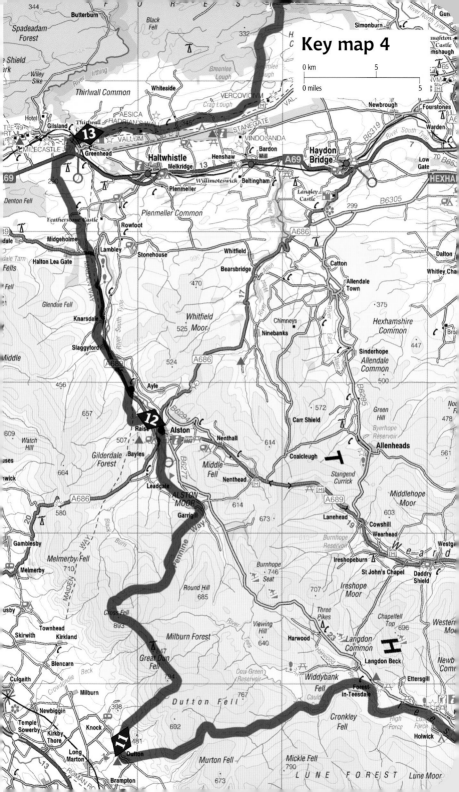

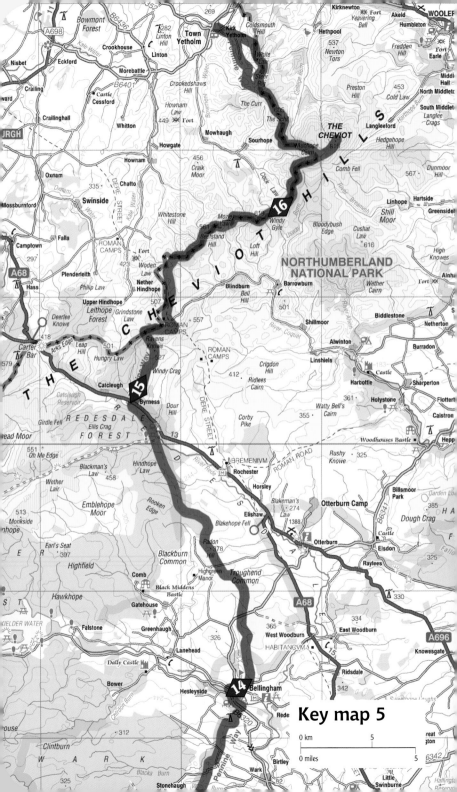

Key map 5

Distance checklist

This list will assist you in calculating the distances between places on the Pennine Way where you may be planning to stay overnight, or in checking your progress along the way.

location	miles	km	location	miles	km
Edale	0	0	Keld	2.8	4.5
Kinder Downfall	4.9	7.9	Tan Hill	4.0	6.4
A57 Snake Road	4.3	6.9	Trough Heads	5.3	8.5
Bleaklow Head	2.3	3.7	Bowes	3.2	5.1
Crowden	4.5	7.2	[A66 (Pasture End)		
Black Hill	4.3	6.9	route avoiding Bowes]	1.2	1.9
A635	1.7	2.7	Pasture End	0	0
Wessenden Reservoir	1.9	3.1	Baldersdale (Blackton)	3.6	5.8
Standedge (A62)	3.1	5.0	[Bowes/Baldersdale]		
M62 crossing	4.4	7.1	Bowes Loop	5.8	9.3
Warland Reservoir	4.9	7.9	Middleton	6.0	9.7
Stoodley Pike	3.1	5.0	Saur Hill/Langdon Beck	7.7	12.4
A646 (for Hebden Bridge)	2.4	3.9	Dufton	12.3	19.8
Walshaw Dean Reservoirs	6.3	10.1	Garrigill	15.8	25.4
Ponden	4.4	7.1	Alston	3.9	6.3
Cowling	4.6	7.4	Slaggyford	5.0	8.0
Lothersdale	2.5	4.0	Greenhead	10.9	17.5
Thornton-in-Craven	4.4	7.1	Steel Rigg/Once Brewed	6.6	10.6
Gargrave	4.3	6.9	Bellingham	14.5	23.3
Malham	6.3	10.1	Byrness	14.7	23.6
Malham Tarn	3.3	5.3	Chew Green	4.9	7.9
Pen-y-ghent	8.0	12.9	Clennell Street		
Horton in Ribblesdale	3.1	5.0	(for Cocklawfoot)	8.8	14.2
Cam Fell	6.4	10.3	Kirk Yetholm (high level)	11.0	17.7
Dodd Fell	3.0	4.8	Kirk Yetholm (low level)	11.3	18.2
Hawes	4.3	6.9	Kirk Yetholm		
Great Shunner Fell	6.2	10.0	(detour to The Cheviot) +	2.3	3.7
Thwaite	3.3	5.3			

The wind whistling through moorland grasses on the descent into Middleton-in-Teesdale – one of the finest ends to a day on the Way.

Swaledale. Sigh. The sort of idyllic Yorkshire Dales scenery that continues to burn brightly in your mind when you're back up on those moody Pennine moors.

Introduction

Why walk the Pennine Way?

Good question. 'You won't come across me anywhere along the Pennine Way,' writes Alfred Wainwright at the end his 1968 guidebook, *Pennine Way Companion*. 'I've had enough of it.'

The famous fell-walker wasn't alone in his views. 'If this book should in some small way encourage people to take up walking themselves,' says Barry Pilton in his hilarious account of walking the Way, *One Man And His Bog*, 'then the author suggests that they read the book again more carefully.'

I'm not trying to put you off walking the Pennine Way. Quite the opposite. It wouldn't after all help sell many copies of this lovingly produced little book you're holding. But you should know that you're thinking about attempting the Big One. When it comes to the UK's National Trails, the Pennine Way is the original, the classic, the daddy; it's the oldest, roughest and toughest of them all.

That should have put off the day-trippers and dilettantes. Still reading? Good. Well, come a little closer my friend. You clearly have guts and courage.

The Pennine Way is 268 miles (431 km) of trail, mostly along the top of the Pennines, the backbone of England as they're often called. The legendary path leads from Edale in Derbyshire's rugged Peak District, through the glorious Yorkshire Dales and along the stirring Hadrian's Wall to the underrated Cheviots and Kirk Yetholm (don't worry, no one else has heard of it either) in Scotland. It is without question some of the wildest, remotest and best upland walking in England.

The route tiptoes through landscapes that inspired great writers, such as the Brontës, William Wordsworth and Charles Kingsley. It's a history lesson on northern England, including insights into the Bronze Age, the

Romans, Vikings, Normans, industrialisation, mining, farming and more. It's a fascinating geological field trip. It's a tour of cosy pubs, of welcoming cafés and of numerous charming villages you've probably never heard of but may never want to leave. It's a good chance to meet like-minded people. But most of all it's a walk through life-affirming natural beauty.

You'll be tramping your muddy boots across the bleakly beautiful gritstone plateaux and melancholy moorlands, up and down secret wind-tickled dales, along rugged ridges with endless views and big big skies, past limestone splendour sculptured by Norse gods, following singing rivers past crashing waterfalls, through wildflower-strewn meadows, up stout mountains and many more lonely and dreamy wild places.

If you like ticking things off, the Way includes England's highest waterfall above ground (Hardraw Force), the highest pub (Tan Hill Inn), the coldest place in the country (Cross Fell), the highest road (Great Dun Fell), the longest canal (Leeds and Liverpool), the highest, deepest and longest canal tunnel (Standedge Tunnel) and one of the Yorkshire Three Peaks (Pen-y-ghent). That's not forgetting totemic Kinder Scout, the compelling yet terrifying chasm of High Cup and 8 miles (12 km) along Hadrian's Wall. Sixty-one per cent of the Way is in National Parks (Northumberland, as well as the Peak and the Dales) and it strides through the North Pennines Area of Outstanding Natural Beauty, two large National Nature Reserves and 20 Sites of Special Scientific Interest. Fans of Harry Potter, Wallace and Gromit, *Robin Hood: Prince of Thieves* and even *Last of the Summer Wine* (well someone must be?) will find places of interest too.

Those who complete the hallowed 268 miles become Pennine Wayfarers, an elite band of lonesome bog-trotters. To have walked the Way is to have achieved something only fellow Wayfarers can fully understand. The experiences – good and bad, but overwhelmingly good – never leave you. It gives a sense of accomplishment no one can diminish and few things can equal. In fact, for want of an equivalent trial afterwards, some simply walk it again. And again. Twelve times is the most I've heard of. There's a touching sense of ephemeral community along the walk, recorded in the visitors' books as you go.

On a personal note, the Way proved to me that, despite Britain's pandemic of cars, tarmac and things that beep, you can still escape all that and in northern England find wild, remote and plain beautiful places, offering a giddy sense of liberation. And that's a very fine thing to find.

However, thanks in part to the likes of Wainwright and Pilton, the Pennine Way does have something of a reputation. The myths include relentless rain, over-crowding, that the path is one big hiker-swallowing quagmire, and that it used to be better, you know, back in the day. Aside from the fact that it can rain in the

Pennines, as it can anywhere else, and, yes, because of the blanket peat in some areas it can be soggy underfoot, none of that is true.

New flagstones (not too many, only over the worst bits) mean the Way isn't the bog-fest it was in Wainwright's day. In fact, the path is better than ever, yet ironically there are fewer walkers than ever. Hikers have been lured by other trails, which are usually more crowded and less wild. That's excellent news for the rest of us. Now is the best time to walk the Pennine Way. This is its heyday.

Britain's oldest National Trail is for the more committed hiker. It can be tough at times. It may well give you blisters, it may well soak you to the skin and the squelching noise could stay with you for days afterwards. But it's a small price to pay – and will add to the sense of achievement. The Pennine Way is a thrilling romp, a deeply satisfying trail, a walk like no other. It could well be one of the best things you ever do.

Day 10: the River Tees has all sorts of party tricks up its sleeve, starting with Low Force (second waterfall).

History of the Pennine Way

There probably wouldn't be a Pennine Way if it wasn't for Tom Stephenson. Stephenson was a journalist and keen walker who would later serve for 21 years as the first full-time secretary of the Ramblers' Association. He was an autodidact, a teetotaller and a dogged intellectual with an amazing memory for facts and dates. Stephenson was also a deeply principled chap and a conscientious objector in the First World War, spending two years in prison as a result.

In 1935 two American girls wrote to the *Daily Herald* newspaper asking for advice on a walking holiday in England. Was there anything here like the Appalachian Trail in the US, they wondered? The short answer was no. Stephenson quickly recognised that the remote wilds of the 'lonely entrancing' Pennines were an excellent place for a long-distance trail and put forward the idea in the same

newspaper. 'Wanted – a long green trail' was the headline, and he called for 'A Pennine Way from the Peak to the Cheviots'. Secretly he hoped to use the path as an excuse to open up the moorlands of the Peak District and South Pennines, much of which was out of bounds to walkers at the time. It's hard to imagine today, but Kinder Scout and surrounding moors where strictly the preserve of grouse-shooting only.

Both of Stephenson's wishes would happen, but he would fight for another 30 years for the Pennine Way to exist. In 1948 he led MPs on a walk from Teesdale to High Cup, then Cross Fell to Hadrian's Wall, to try to convince them of the idea. The project gained ministerial approval in 1951 but it took a further 14 years to open up the 70 miles (113 km) of new paths to complete the route.

Britain's first National Trail opened on 24 April 1965, 33 years to the day after Benny Rothman led the legendary Kinder Mass Trespass (for more, see page 31). Two thousand walkers gathered at Malham Moor, in the Yorkshire Dales, for the Way's birth. Stephenson would later pen a guidebook for the walk, the first official one, as would Wainwright (see below).

Stephenson got his bigger wish too, as in 1949 the National Parks and Access to the Countryside Act opened up England's glorious countryside for the likes of you and me to get wet and muddy in. Pay a thought or two to the great man as you walk along his Way. If, for some unforeseen reason, the Pennine Way ever needed to be renamed, it should rightly be called the Stephenson Way.

From a hiking legend to a football legend, and perhaps the most famous person to have walked a respectable amount of the Pennine Way is Brian Clough. The much-celebrated manager walked a week on the southern half of the trail in the summer of 1977 in support of fundraising Nottinghamshire miners.

Tom Stephenson: without this great man the Pennine Way might never have existed.

Wainwright and the Pennine Way

Alfred Wainwright, or AW, gained fame through his pictorial guides to walks in the Lake District. But it was a hike across the Pennines in 1938 that led to his first walking book. Even if it wasn't published for nearly 50 years.

As the Second World War beckoned, the future guidebook guru escaped the twin stresses of Adolf Hitler's Germany and his passionless marriage to walk from Settle to Hadrian's Wall up the eastern side of the Pennines, then back again down the west. This was back in the day when you could seemingly knock on a stranger's door and be cheerily put up for the night. On his return he scribbled up his story and stuck it in a drawer. Later, when Wainwright was famous for his illustrated guides to Lakeland, a casual comment to his publisher brought around the publication of *A Pennine Journey* in 1986.

The book is both a snapshot of a compelling moment of world history and of the 31-year-old Lancastrian, with his love of the outdoors (and some of his more primitive social views) clear throughout. A blue plaque at the Settle Railway Station, in the guidebook writer's trademark font, marks his journey and the Wainwright Society has produced a guidebook (*A Pennine Journey: From Settle to Hadrian's Wall in Wainwright's Footsteps*) for a route he may have taken today, considering road and rights-of-way changes.

The arch rambler and the Pennines were reunited in 1966 when he began researching his guidebook, *Pennine Way Companion* (1968) – which, idiosyncratically, reads from back to front. The nit-picking rambler pointed out that if the Pennine Way was true to its name it should really lie along the Pennine Range exclusively, taking in the Derbyshire Dales and ending east of Carlisle – though he admitted his were the opinions of a 'chronic purist'. Wainwright talked of the 'masculine grandeur' of the 'simple' and 'sturdy' Way, compared to the feminine charms of the Coast to Coast Walk. He preferred the latter, as the Way and the Wainwright didn't get along.

Alfred Wainwright

'Well, I'm glad that's finished, I must say,' he writes in his Conclusion. His misadventures included being rescued from sinking into a bog on Black Hill, a lot of rain and freezing gales. One gale 'so shrivelled some of the body organs necessary for a full and enjoyable life that I feared they were perished forever'.

He was unlucky with the weather. 'I suppose the Pennine Way never dries out,' he said. 'It never did for me.' His tone softens, however. 'In a macabre sort of way I enjoyed [the rain].' He tells would-be Wayfarers: 'There will be days of bright sunshine too and moments of fun; many interesting experiences and a vision of beauty in desolate places will be your reward. If you start don't give up or you will give up at difficulties all your life.' He adds: 'I hope you enjoy it, I really do. In a way I feel sorry for you.'

He was in good enough spirits to shout a half pint of ale in Kirk Yetholm's Border Hotel to any Wayfarer who finished the walk in one go, which ultimately cost him around £15,000 (the pub still offers gratis halves).

This guidebook is full of Wainwright's views, partly because they're often so well observed, and if they're not they're often amusing, intentionally or otherwise. Plus, you'll find many a fellow Wayfarer quoting Wainwright at you. So you'll have a few choice soundbites to quote back.

Pennine landscapes and geology

The name 'Pennines' is illegitimate and an act of 'literary forgery', said Tom Stephenson. In 1747 a young English professor claimed to have discovered a 14th-century book describing Britain in Roman times, including mountains called the Pennine Alps. The book didn't exist, but his idea may have come from William Camden, an Elizabethan historian, who in 1586 wrote that northern England had a range of hills 'like as Apennine in Italy'.

The Pennines aren't really a mountain chain, though, rather a broad uplift of hills that form a watershed. Rainwater falling here turns either east or west before making its way back out to sea.

The Pennines started to form around 300 million years ago, in the semi-tropical Carboniferous period. They've been built, broadly speaking, in three geological sections stacked on top of each other, not unlike a lasagne. Limestone provides the skeletal base, though it isn't openly visible until Malham. An enormous river system brought the Yoredale rocks (the pasta) – less pure limestone, shales and sandstones – and plonked them on top of the limestone. On top of these, especially on the bigger summits such as Kinder Scout and Cross Fell, is a layer of Millstone Grit (the cheese). Volcanoes and the Ice Age have both done their fair share of sculpting too.

The Way begins in idyllic Edale in the heart of the Peak District, the world's second most visited National Park. You're soon up on the gritstone Kinder plateau and across the eerie moonscape of Bleaklow, then over more moors, the once-notorious Black Hill and the lonely, peculiar grit rock formations of Blackstone Edge. Rambling by reservoirs leads down into the verdant Calder Valley, then up and through the wind-brushed moors of Brontë country, before a pastoral stroll through the Aire Gap leads to the Yorkshire Dales. 'At Malham geology hits you between the eyes,' wrote Wainwright and a glorious glacio-karst (limestone) landscape unfolds. You also meet your first real mountain, Pen-y-ghent, a peculiar beast forged by layers of strong sandstone and limestone with weaker shales. The Way climbs over open fells, follows a Roman road to handsome Hawes and the hefty, wind-hammered gritstone plateaux of Great Shunner Fell, before the beautiful meadows of Swaledale.

The North Pennines Area of Outstanding Natural Beauty (AONB) has some of the highest and wildest moorland in England. From here, around halfway, the walk becomes more remote. But first a series of valleys, with world-renowned wild flowers and tuneful rivers springing up where the Alston Block (a succession of Carboniferous sedimentary rocks which form the North Pennines) has been rammed by a large sheet of dolerite, forming the epic Whin Sill. The geological mash-up has produced joyful waterfalls on the River Tees and the compelling abyss of High Cup, the Way's finest moment. From Dufton you climb and climb until Cross Fell, the highest point in England outside the Lake District, is breathlessly reached.

Then it's valleys and meadows, across the bleak Blenkinsopp Common and into the unsung Northumberland National Park, and 8 atmospheric miles along Hadrian's Wall's best bit. Silent forests and eerie moorland lead to Byrness, the gateway to the dramatic Cheviot massif, shaped by volcanoes and composed of igneous rocks of the Devonian age.

Humans have played their part in shaping the Pennines, most markedly through mining. Relics pepper the route, from an industry that dates to the Romans. Farming has had a sizable impact in re-shaping the landscape, too, as have ancient trade routes, Bronze Age forts, Roman forts, walls and roads. Likewise, the Vikings and Normans have left physical and place-name markers.

Pennine flora and fauna

Half of the Pennine Way is across open moorland, so heather and peat feature prominently. Heather moorland may not seem particularly special to us Brits, but we have around 75 per cent of the world's total, so to everyone else it's a rare habitat. The most common species is ling, though bell heather appears regularly too. In August and September the moors turn into enchanting seas of purple.

Peat is a similarly underrated flora and some of the black gooey stuff you'll be walking on could be as ancient as 7,000 years old. Back then most of the Pennines were covered in trees, but Neolithic woodland-clearance exposed the ground to more increased rainfall, which meant minerals were washed away and the surface became waterlogged, making it impossible for bacteria to rot the vegetation. A layer of black, undecayed plant debris accumulated, at about an inch (2.5 cm) a century. For the past 5,000 years the Peak moors have been carpeted in peat,

or blanket bog, to an average depth of 3.25 feet (1 metre). In places such as Bleaklow and Black Hill the peat cover has worn away to leave 'hags', steep-faced islands where the whole history of post-glacial Britain is visible as a multi-layered profile.

Waterlogged mires are very acidic and poor in nutrients, so few plants thrive, sphagnum (bog) moss being an exception.

The High Pennines are also characterised by tussocky moor grass and bog cotton. Other moorland regulars include bilberry, crowberry, deer-grass, sundew and cloudberry, an Arctic refugee. Getting to know cottongrass, which flecks the moors white in summer, could mean keeping your feet dry (see page 38). In wetter spots you can find bog asphodel, marsh pennywort and marsh thistle. In slightly lower areas you might see cowslips, bloody cranesbill and self-heal.

The beautiful meadows of Swaledale are famous for their wild flowers (best seen in spring and early summer), while Upper Teesdale's uniquely ancient habitat has produced rare flowers of world renown (see page 119). Teesdale's biggest star is the

Classic Swaledale: a sea of bewitching wild flowers includes buttercups, wood sorrel and bloody cranesbill.

Nice beard, pal: if you're lucky you may see feral goats in the Cheviots.

there's a chance to see roe deer, Pennine foxes, mountain hares, otter, mink, stoat, bats and red squirrels (the latter possible near Hawes, though more likely near Dufton and in Kielder Forest further north), while feral goats are sometimes spotted in the Cheviots. Startling eggar moths (page 105) and rare Emperor moths (more on page 164) are worth looking out for. Sightings of frogs, lizards and snakes are all entirely possible. Also, though they're not wild, spring is wonderful for lambs.

Birdwatchers are in for a treat. The Pennines are one of the best places in Europe to see breeding waders in the spring and early summer. The heathery moors are often home to grouse (think Donald Duck laughing), usually red, but black too, in the North Pennines. The South Pennine moors are England's most important habitat for the twite, or Pennine finch (even if they are a little drab in appearance). Merlins, Britain's smallest falcon, can sometimes be seen on the moors, as can the short-eared owl. Curlews will definitely be heard. They're the symbol of Northumberland National Park and Stephenson thought they'd make an apt icon for the Way itself. Golden plovers, dunlins and snipe shouldn't be hard to spy. You'll probably hear skylarks, while linnets like to nest in juniper scrub. Lapwings are more likely in higher pasture, while the reservoirs attract swans and other wildfowl.

spring gentian, which produces a five-petalled, vivid blue flower. Another rarity, the Teesdale violet, grows on broken limey ground and is smaller and pinker than other violets. Bird's-eye primrose is another beauty (look for pink and the pastel shades). The mountain pansy (yellow with brown lines), alpine bistort (white or pink on long stalks, also found on the Tibetan plateau) are worth keeping an eye out for. The spring sandwort and the Yorkshire sandwort are about, as is the excellently named bog sandwort. Pen-y-ghent is famous for its purple saxifrage in April, while nearby Hull Pot hosts yellow mountain saxifrage in June.

Of course, many more common but no-less charming plants, flowers and beguiling natural smells pepper the route, such as wild garlic and thyme, ferns, tormentil, thrift, harebells and more. Also, look out for orchid species in quarries and on hillsides. Where relevant in this book, flora you're likely to spot is pointed out in the route description.

There's a good chance of encountering some of Britain's wild things, too. The quieter you are, the more you're likely to see, and dusk and dawn are prime times. Apart from the more obvious mammals,

Birdlife is also plentiful in the valleys and warblers, pied, yellow and grey wagtails are all likely to be seen as well as heard. Likewise kingfishers, dippers and sandpipers by rivers. Near cliffs look for kestrels, peregrine falcons and jackdaws. And you may even see eagles in the Cheviots. Good bird-sighting spots are mentioned throughout the route description.

Perhaps the most curious wildlife sighting of all, however, will be the Pennine Wayfarer: wide-eyed, unkempt, mud-caked and smelly, these are strange creatures indeed.

How to walk the Pennine Way

Some complete the Pennine Way in 12 days, others in 12 years. It's unlikely, however, that anyone will get from Edale to Kirk Yetholm as fast as Mike Hartley. In July 1989, the fell-runner ran the 268 miles in a Herculean 2 days, 17 hours, 20 minutes and 15 seconds. He halted only twice, including to knock back fish and chips in Alston. On average, most one-go walkers take a massively more sensible 16–19 days.

For the ultimate sense of satisfaction, carrying all your own kit on one continuous foot journey is the way to go. But neither Tom Stephenson, Alfred Wainwright nor this guidebook writer (though he's blaming the birth of his daughter) walked the Pennine Way in one go. Of the estimated 1,800 people who complete the walk each year, an increasing number are what in the US they call 'section hikers'.

The Pennine Way is designed to run south–north, which generally keeps the weather at your back and saves arguably the best section till last. But there's no reason why it can't be walked north–south and, while this guide is designed south–north, it should work almost as well backwards.

The 16 stages suggested here are based on a sensible pace, averaging 18 miles (29 km) a day. The sections aren't set in stone and there are often good alternative stop-offs, so tailor the walk to suit your preferences.

Walk in spring for daffodils and lambs; in summer for longer days, more sunshine, but more people on the trail, or early summer for the explosion of wild flowers in Swaledale and Upper Teesdale; walk in early autumn for purple moors (in September, but August too); and in winter to get the Way all to yourself, though some facilities may be unavailable. Generally the best time to walk the Way is between April and September, but be prepared for rain, wind and cold all year round.

You can pay a company to transport your luggage each day (see page 187), which means less stress on your back, but more stress on the environment.

What does it cost to walk the Pennine Way? As a loose example, staying at youth hostels wherever possible would probably cost upwards of £40 a day. A lot will depend on your choice of accommodation . . .

Accommodation

When it comes to accommodation, it's largely a case of tailoring the walk to your tastes and budget. A small, localised industry lives off the trail, offering largely excellent services in return. There's a good deal of flexibility along most of the route, but in smaller places (such as Crowden, Standedge, Tan Hill, Ickornshaw, Cowling, Greenhead and Byrness) accommodation is limited.

The cheapest option is wild camping, which in England is permissible only with the agreement of the landowner. However, there's a tradition of backpackers arriving in the evening, breaking camp early and leaving no trace of their stay. Good practice includes: no open fires, carrying everything out that you brought in and making toilet at least 50 metres away from watercourses. Wild camping on National Trust properties is strictly prohibited.

However, while wild camping can be exhilarating, it offers little to local economies along the way. This part of England isn't especially prosperous and some satisfaction can be gained from chipping in, however little. Also, Natural England ask you to use formal campsites whenever possible and there are plenty of those on route. It often costs as little as £6 for a site and use of toilet and shower facilities.

Youth hostels are available in the majority of logical stop-off points and cost from around £15 for a dorm bed. Most offer evening meals (up to £10), cooked - breakfasts (around £5) and packed lunches (around £5 – many B&Bs will offer packed lunches too), plus the chance to swap tips and compare blisters with other walkers. They're cheaper for YHA members.

A lower-cost, if rarer, alternative is bunk houses. This is usually just a roof over a wooden sleeping platform or bunk and toilet facilities, from around £6. You'll need your own sleeping bag and sleeping mat. There are also a few opportunities to sleep in bothies (refuge huts) along the Pennine Way. They're free, but basic. Tidy up after yourself, and there's a tradition of leaving a small gift for the next visitors.

B&Bs, guesthouses, hotels and pubs offering accommodation (all around £25-60) feature in most villages and towns en route and some are surprisingly plush.

Some walkers like to book a year in advance, others turn up on the day. For accommodation in the remoter areas, it

may be as well to book ahead. If you're in the latter group, remember that accommodation gets busier at weekends and busier still in the summer holidays (July–August). Hostels get booked up too, sometimes by school parties at weekends. The Cheviots is a tricky section as there are no accommodation options on the Way between Days 15 and 16, but a bit of planning will see you right (see page 172 for alternatives).

This book is organised into sections which end with accommodation and sustenance options, so there's not usually any need to carry more than lunch and energy snacks if you're using accommodation. In more remote or small places (such as Standedge), if accommodation doesn't offer evening meals they'll sometimes drive you to a local pub that does. Campers may want to carry about two

The legendary Tan Hill Inn should provide one of the most memorable nights on the Way.

days' food on average and note that cooking gas is hard to come by.

In the route descriptions, if a town or village is labelled as having a 'wide selection' of accommodation, it means four or more options.

For accommodation listings and contact information, visit the official trail website, which has a helpful interactive accommodation map. The Pennine Way Association also does an accommodation guide. Contact details for both are given in the Useful Information section, page 187.

Some guiding baggage courier companies will book accommodation for you (see page 187), while local tourist information and National Park centres can also help. The relevant ones are listed on pages 187–88.

Transport

If you're walking the Way in one go, transport is fairly straightforward. Edale is well served by trains from Manchester and Sheffield, and buses; Kirk Yetholm less so, but it still has regular buses (except on Sundays when there are none) going on to Kelso for further connections. A taxi is another possibility (see page 187).

Elsewhere, trains cross the Pennines only at Hebden Bridge, Gargrave, Garsdale Station (near Hawes) and Horton in Ribblesdale. However, buses go to most places. Generally speaking, the further north you go, the fewer transport options there are, especially after Greenhead.

The best place to start planning your transport is Traveline: contact details and more information on page 187.

Preparation and equipment

The Pennine Way is a serious undertaking and it would be unwise for the trail to be anyone's first multi-day walk if attempted in one go. Because the summits are broad rather than brief, weather here can be more severe than in the Lake District or north Wales, and even in summer temperatures on the hilltops can be zero degrees. Though frostbite and altitude sickness won't trouble you (at least until you re-tell your adventure), with a total ascent of 36,823 feet (11,224 metres) you will have climbed considerably more than an Everest climber. However, people aged eight to eighty enjoy the walk and it doesn't require an army-esque training regime beforehand. But the fitter you are, the more you'll enjoy it.

You don't need to spend thousands of pounds on brightly coloured kit either – Wainwright only ever walked in his tweed suit and leather shoes (but then he did get very wet and miserable). Regardless of the time of year, you should pack for all four seasons and some bits of equipment are key.

The most important item is always boots – make sure they're comfy – and treat your feet like they're royalty (cut nails, deal with blisters asap and whisper sweet nothings to them). Leather boots won't usually dry out fully over night, while new-fangled waterproof socks and gaiters are a good idea. But whatever methods of prevention you try, on some sections the wet stuff will get to your pink little piggies eventually.

The second most important item is a waterproof jacket – make sure it really is waterproof. Your pack must fit well and the lighter it is the happier you'll be.

A minimum first-aid kit should include plasters, pain relief and antiseptic cream at the very least. Take a torch too. Also, don't start the Way with any untested bits of key kit – try it out first.

After the essentials, equipment choices are a personal thing, though going without walking poles is a kamikaze act – for saving yourself from hungry peat bogs if nothing else.

Signposting, navigation and communications

The Pennine Way has many surfaces, from the usually very welcome flagstones, moorland (bog enthusiasts will not be disappointed) and hillside paths, to very occasional tarmac, stony tracks and wooden walkways (duckboards), plus woodland and riverside sections. Occasionally it's rocky and there's even a spot of scrambling on Pen-y-ghent and by Cauldron Snout. Naturally, the path can be steep, but long stiff climbs are surprisingly rare.

The Way is well signposted most of the way (look for the acorn symbol too 🌰) and flagstones double as a great navigation aid in places. However, the route isn't always obvious, plus foul, view-blocking weather can descend quickly, especially up high. So a compass is essential, as are the skills to use it.

The maps and the route descriptions here should be enough to see you safely along the Way, while GPS references are for points that may be useful or are potentially unclear. It would take hours to input them all into your GPS, so it's best to use them if you ever feel unsure of the exact route. Most people get along fine without a GPS.

If you feel you want full maps, see page 189, but it's a heavy load and you should think about posting them on ahead. Alternatively, Harvey Maps have the whole route on three maps and Footprint Maps do similar – see page 189.

Mobile phones are useful to tell people where you are, contact accommodation and for emergencies. However, coverage is not comprehensive and will depend on your provider. Most phones will have reception approximately three-quarters of the time. Wi-fi reception is similarly unpredictable.

Safety and hazards

The Pennines aren't the Himalayas, but things can still go wrong – and quickly. Navigational hiccups are the most common catalyst for misadventure and they're more likely in bad weather (and when tired), so where possible find a forecast. That said, the weather is notoriously unpredictable. The Pennines receive around 98 inches (2.5 metres) of the wet stuff per annum, and can be very cold and windy even in summer. It's good practice to tell a non-Wayfarer where you're going to be that day. Always carry food, water, warm and waterproof clothes.

If you do find yourself outside your comfort zone in bad weather, the standard advice is to stay where you are – often the clouds will clear and normal service can be resumed. If you're more than one, have a good think before splitting up, as that could make a situation worse. In an emergency, call mountain rescue on 999 (but only in a genuine emergency). If you have a whistle or torch, the general signal for help is six blasts or flashes. If waving for help, use two arms not one (which usually means hello). But worry not: the vast majority of walkers have no real problems – well, apart from blisters.

Blisters should be treated as soon as you feel a hot spot – slap on a plaster or tape. Piercing a blister can lead to infection, but if you do, smother it with antiseptic and apply a plaster or moleskin.

Being wet and cold can mean your body struggles to maintain a normal temperature and there's a risk of hypothermia, which, if unchecked, can be fatal. Find shelter, get warm, imbibe food and drink and get further help.

Stay hydrated and protect your head to avoid heat exhaustion. If you start to feel groggy, try rehydration powders or salts, or (isotonic) sports drinks; salty crisps and other soft drinks can help too. Heatstroke is more serious and can lead to death. A lack of sweat and bad coordination may spell trouble, so get help urgently.

Adder bites are seldom fatal but shouldn't be ignored – immobilise the affected area and seek medical advice. The only other animal that might cause you trouble is the great British cow. With new calves, normally passive cows can get protective, so give them a wide berth and don't get between calves and their mothers. If cattle approach, they'll usually stop before reaching you, so carry on quietly and don't run. If they come very close, step towards them waving your arms and shouting firmly. In the unlikely event you are attacked, report it to the landowner.

Midges can be annoying near Scotland, so insect repellent is a good idea in summer. Treat water from streams and reservoirs before drinking.

Sustainable walking and the Countryside Code

The Pennines have some of England's best-preserved wilderness areas, but these are often fragile and ancient habitats. Animals, such as otters, have recently faced extinction and many species are threatened; even skylarks are rapidly declining. There are lots of things we can do to try to conserve the beautiful things we have left, most of which will be second nature to outdoor types, but they bear repeating.

Leave nothing but footprints and take nothing but pictures, as the mantra goes, and that includes the likes of banana skins and apple cores. Don't be afraid to lead by example and pick up other people's rubbish too. Stay on the main trail whenever possible, especially across farmland. If you find wildlife, lucky you – but don't cause any undue stress, especially if babies are involved. Don't pollute watercourses, leave gates as they are (open or closed), don't light fires and

Stone flagstones are very welcome at times, to keep feet dry but also as navigational aids. They keep the bogs hungry.

don't make unnecessary noise. Use toilets where they're provided, but if you must go in the wild, make it at least 50 metres from watercourses (make a hole and fill it in afterwards). Support local business when possible, likewise public transport, and seriously consider whether you need a baggage courier service. Lecture over.

Dogs, horses and bikes

If you want to bring your best canine buddy along for the tramp, it's vital that you can exercise good control over him. Farmers may not welcome dogs between mid-March and mid-May, which is lambing season. But it's a public right of way and people are allowed to take their dog all year round, as long as it's under control. Be careful around cows, who sometimes go for dogs, in conservation areas (especially around birds) and near other walkers. Some accommodation options are happy to take pets and bootsandpaws.co.uk, which gives advice on walking and visiting places with dogs, may be a good starting point. You may also enjoy Mark Wallington's highly amusing *Pennine Walkies*.

The Pennine Way is not open to cyclists or horseriders, but our four-legged and two-wheeled friends are welcome to try the Pennine Bridleway National Trail. This new 200-mile (322-km) purpose-built route follows old packhorse trails, drover roads and newly created bridleways. The full route will be opened in the summer of 2012, but much is useable already.

The Pennine Way's best bits

Edale to Crowden (Day 1)

The exhilaration of clean boots and fresh socks finally pounding the Pennine Way is matched by the thrill of the wind riffling through hair as you contend with the stirring Kinder Plateau. The Way starts like a Bond film: all action and glory from the off.

Malham to Horton in Ribblesdale (Day 6)

Malham marks the start of glorious limestone country. From the beautiful village itself, the biblical Gordale Scar, Hollywood's Malham Cove, graceful Malham Tarn and a limestone pavement here and there, it's a unique and wondrous day. Plus you get the first real mountain, Pen-y-ghent.

Hawes to Tan Hill (Day 8)

More than any other, today really does feel like walking along the backbone of England. After the Way's most spectacular waterfall (Hardraw Force), it's up on to the marvellous moors and over the behemoth of Great Shunner Fell. Then through cute little Thwaite, along the top of dashing Swaledale and a memorable night at the Tan Hill Inn.

Middleton-in-Teesdale to Dufton (Day 10)

Skipping through flowery meadows, following the playful Tees, Low Force tickles your fancy and High Force tickles you somewhere fancier, before Cauldron

Snout snorts at you. That's a pretty good day by anyone's standards, but the best bit of the whole walk is still to come . . . Plus Dufton's a gem, too.

Dufton to Alston (Day 11)

Mention this leg and veteran Wayfarers emit a knowing chuckle. In good weather the highest part of the Way must be utterly spectacular. It's just that Cross Fell and good weather aren't usually used in the same sentence. A day to remember, either way.

Greenhead to Bellingham (Day 13)

On any other walk Hadrian's Wall would be the highlight, but the Way has so much splendour the Roman wall almost gets forgotten. You march along one of the world's most famous historical sites for 8 miles (12.8 km), with views to match the heady sense of drama.

Byrness to Kirk Yetholm (Days 15 and 16)

Talk about saving the best for last. Two days of walking over the glorious, giant domes of wind-swept volcanic rock, with hardly a soul about. What a finale.

For what it's worth, the often contrary Wainwright listed his highlights as: Kinder Downfall, Gordale Scar (off route), Malham Cove, Hull Pot (off route), Ling Gill, Hardraw Force, High Force, Cauldron Snout, High Cup, the Roman Wall and Hareshaw Linn (off route).

Pennine Way

High Force (Day 10): where the Tees takes a reckless but joyous leap off a 70-foot (21-metre) dolerite cliff. Wainwright called it 'The greatest waterfall in the country'.

Edale to Crowden

via the Kinder Plateau and Bleaklow Head
16 miles (26 km)

Ascent 2,430 feet (740 metres)
Descent 2,560 feet (780 metres)
Highest point Bleaklow Head: 2,076 feet (633 metres)
Lowest point Crowden: 656 feet (200 metres)

It would be uncharacteristic and perhaps even a little bit sneaky of the Pennine Way to start you off gently. Instead it charges out of its corner and bops you square on the nose – it wants to see what you're made of.

Day 1 includes the route's second-longest ascent, one of the most notorious spots for topographical embarrassment – Bleaklow Head – and a section bearing the devil's name (rarely a good sign, unless of course your name is Lucifer). That said, in terms of scenery, this ranks in the Way's Top Five. If the weather's half-decent, you're in for a panoramic feast.

A gentle amble through fields becomes a steep climb. Up on the plateau, the compelling journey through the savage beauty of the Peak District's gritstone moors and peat groughs is mostly flat walking – though you'll need to pay attention to navigation – followed by a long but enjoyable descent into tiny Crowden.

Crowden has no facilities other than a youth hostel and campsite, which do provide food, and there are no lunch options en route either. So stock up in Edale – and perhaps for the next leg too, as Standedge is similarly bereft.

Things to look out for

1 The Old Nag's Head This pub, the semi-official starting point of the Pennine Way, does well out of the walk, but not without good reason. Inside the cosy, walker-friendly establishment (there's a different bar for locals) you'll find a wood fire, real ale and tasty nosh. The stone building dates back to 1577.

2 Edale Months of reading and daydreaming about the Pennine Way may have elevated Edale to a kind of Valhalla in some minds. Scenically it doesn't disappoint, with the Peak District's finest standing to attention like guards on all sides. Even if you're champing at the bit to get going, there may be some reluctance to leave this lovely little village of cosy pubs and tinkling streams. Wainwright snorted that there was 'no logical reason' for the Way to start here, but it feels like there are some pretty good ones, actually.

5 Jacob's Ladder Part of today's walk used to be an important pan-Pennine trade route, where wool and salt journeyed in either direction. Ponies took a long zigzagging path up on to the moor, but, so the story goes, Jacob Marshall would send his faithful steed the long way and take a shortcut up the steepest slope, where he sat and watched the others sweating away, while smugly smoking his pipe. His route has become Jacob's Ladder and you'll probably come to curse it.

6 Edale Cross The age of the Edale Cross, found just a few minutes off the route between Jacob's Ladder and Edale Rocks, is unknown. The ancient monument could be medieval, but more likely once marked a boundary of landownership or was a packhorse-route waymarker. Nevertheless, it looks suitably mysterious and stands in an atmospherically lonely spot.

Kinder Scout Few, if any, English mountains are more symbolic than the Peak District's highest, oft nicknamed The Peak. In 1932 around 400 walkers, led by the 20-year-old Benny Rothman, scuffled with gamekeepers to mass trespass on the summit in protest against limited access to the countryside. Though its significance has perhaps been overplayed, many see it as a turning point and 'right to roam' legislation followed, though not before a four-month stint behind bars for Rothman and four others. We owe those courageous law-breakers, and the incident is celebrated in songs by Ewan McColl and Chumbawamba.

The Pennine Way used to go directly over Kinder Scout, but owing to erosion it has been re-routed to travel along the edge of the plateau.

10 Devil's Dike The Way crosses an ancient path, Doctor's Gate, with several stories attached to it. According to one, an alchemist, or perhaps doctor, sold his soul to the Devil and tried to win it back in a horse race along Doctor's Gate. By leaping the Dike – a wide ditch in the peat – just ahead of the Devil, the doc managed to put water between them and break the spell. Devil's Dike could be that, or it could have marked an ancient boundary, perhaps Saxon. It could also have been dug in the

13th century by the monks of Basingwerk Abbey, Flintshire. Or all three. Or none of the above. At worst, the Dike can feel like a labyrinth of trenches, or groughs as they're named locally. Or, as Barry Pilton put it in *One Man and His Bog*, 'like stumbling around inside a giant's crotch'. It's a unique section of the Way, a spag bol of weird and wonderful shapes.

12 Bleaklow Head 'Nobody loves Bleaklow,' proclaimed Alfred Wainwright in his guidebook. He thought the hill an 'unfriendly and cheerless place'. But after 'a stinging rebuke from a Huddersfield man', Wainwright was forced to reconsider, just a bit. 'I suppose everything, however unattractive, is loved by someone,' he said begrudgingly in *Wainwright on the Pennine Way*. 'Low' is derived from the Old English *hlaew*, meaning burial ground or hill. Bleaklow's terrain, of peat wastelands, sand and gritstone boulders, has more than a hint of the apocalyptic about it, emphasised by nearby wreckage of an American B-29 Superfortress aircraft, the prophetically named Overexposed, that crashed here in 1948, with the death of all 13 on board.

That's not the only sad news about Bleaklow. Along with Kinder and Black Hill, the habitat here has been classed as degraded peat bog. Pollution, grazing and hiking boots have taken their toll on the fragile landscape and the peat's water table has dropped, leaving it dry and vulnerable to further erosion. What exactly this means ecologically is unclear, but the terrain is changing and there's concern that the peat bog, which stores carbon, will start releasing it. The habitat is being carefully managed, however, and the increase of sphagnum moss in recent years is cause for optimism.

In good weather you can glimpse Pen-y-ghent to the north, a week's walk away, and sometimes even Mount Snowdon in Wales, far off in the west.

Route description

The **Old Nags Head** **1** in **Edale** **2** is generally seen as the start of the Way. Take the signposted path directly to your left (as you look at the pub), which climbs gently along a sunken path. Turn left over a stile and follow the stone slabs as the route passes through pleasant pastures, soon running parallel with Broadlee-Bank Tor.

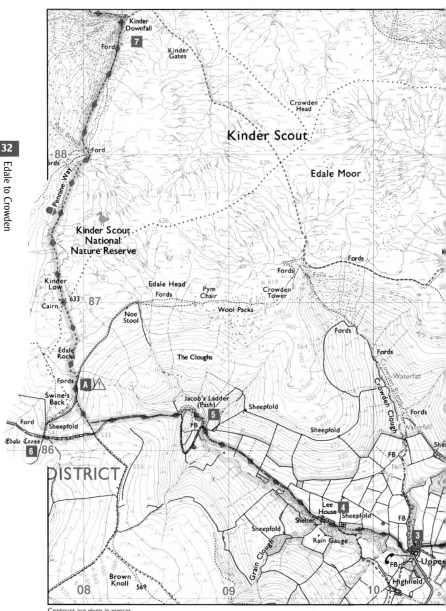

Contours are given in metres
The vertical interval is 10m

The attendant shrubbery changes from hawthorn, ash and holly to rowan and birch, and views of alluring peaks, including the 'shivering mountain' (Mam Tor) frame a picturesque valley. The mini-utopia will likely be remembered fondly once you're up on the windy, desolate moorland above.

The path is easy to follow and you'll soon find a bench, which has arrived too early for a justified rest, but the charming views on offer may seem too good to pass by (go on, treat yourself). There's some inspiring poetry on the bench too.

The track starts to swing south-west and downhill into Upper Booth **3** (the farm has a campsite and a camping barn). Turn right along a metalled road, crossing the river in the shade of some sessile oak, wych-elm, alder, rowan and sycamore trees. Through a gate the track leads to Lee Farm, past an information shelter **4** and north-west to a packhorse bridge. **Jacob's Ladder 5** is a mission you've already chosen to accept. It's time to tighten your backpack straps.

As the climb becomes less steep, you pass a giant cairn and come to a fork. Left is a 10-minute detour, through a gate to **Edale Cross 6**; right is the main route. (From Edale Cross you can simply retrace your steps or take a more roundabout route, marked on the map, to reunite with the official path at a large cairn.) Then bear left along the stone surfaced path to a large cairn **A**, GPS 53° 22.241 01° 49.009, and left again towards the curious stone outcrop of Edale Rocks. The wind has probably already let you know you're finally on the peaty moorland plateau – both desolate and forbidding, yet curiously compelling. Now it feels like you're really on the Pennine Way.

Take a final look at the Vale of Edale, the pass to the right, east, of the rocks and follow the vague path through a lunar landscape of gritty pebbles, black peat and rocks. There are some cairns, but if you lose the path temporarily, just keep roughly to the edge. You'll want to anyway – the views into the valley are worth a peep.

Keep to the left of Kinder Low's triangulation point, GPS 53° 21.997 01° 50.159 (2,076 feet/633 metres), and continue to bear north-north-east along the stony edge. Red Brook, which you soon cross, is an area popular with mountain hares, curlew and golden plovers.

Like an old rocker refusing to put down his Fender, Kinder Downfall **7** is living on former glories. It's easy to imagine the glacial water roaring by in the waterfall's prime. Today, while it sometimes still puts on a show and blows backwards on itself, it can also be an apologetic little trickle.

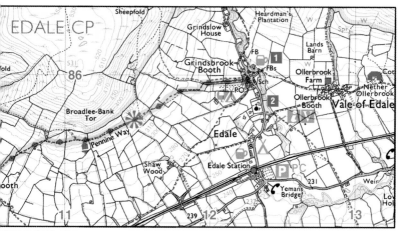

ontours are given in metres
The vertical interval is 10m

The path seems to evaporate here, but after some rock-hopping across to the other side, GPS 53° 23.822 01°52.586, stick again to the rocky edge as the route bears north-west.

Along here the vegetation is spare, with some crowberry and bilberry, and rocks have been sculpted into intriguing shapes. You may get attractive views of the Kinder Reservoir below and (the less attractive) Manchester in the distance.

Continuing along the edge you eventually reach a cairn before a sharp descent to a gravel path. Ignore the stone-slab path to the left. Climb again, going straight over at a crossroads. Close to here is a Stone Age flint factory , where the sharp stones were crafted to use as arrow and spear heads and other tools.

The Way is on slab stones again to the cairn on top of Mill Hill, GPS 53° 24.632 01° 54.567, which caused Wainwright to remark aptly, 'There's no mill and not much hill'. The route is clear as it turns right, north-east, and takes you to a broad crest, often flushed pink by the cottongrass. The path bears a more easterly direction approaching Glead Hill, then north-east again towards Featherhead Moss B.

The ever-cheery Wainwright thought, 'Nobody has a kind word to say about Featherhead Moss, and no wonder, for it does nothing to earn it.' But in the sunshine, with the triumphant Kinder Plateau to my right, glorious sweeps of wild landscape all around and the wind trying to make off with my hair, I felt immensely

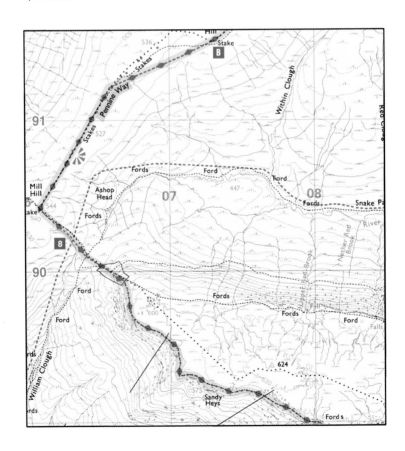

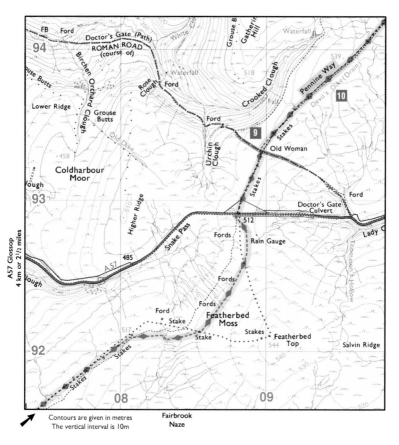

Contours are given in metres
The vertical interval is 10m

Fairbrook
Naze

happy and liberated on this stretch. I was on the Pennine Way. And it was great.

That said, I soon saw the surreal sight of cars motoring across the moor. The A57 Snake Pass is ahead, a road that's usually first to shut when extreme weather arrives. If you think you can hear Donald Duck laughing at you around here, it's more likely to be grouse, before they rocket out of the undergrowth nearby as if on fire.

Cross over the incongruous tarmac, likewise Doctor's Gate **9**, which is marked on maps as a Roman Road though most remaining flagstones are of medieval origin, and follow stone slabs to **Devil's Dike 10**. The Dike has a reputation for getting Wayfarers lost, but it's deceptively easy to follow and a unique feature to enjoy. There are intermittent cairns, welcome stone waymarkers and slabbed sections.

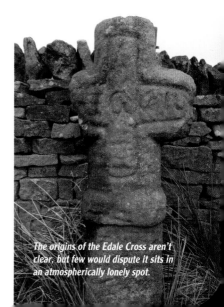

The origins of the Edale Cross aren't clear, but few would dispute it sits in an atmospherically lonely spot.

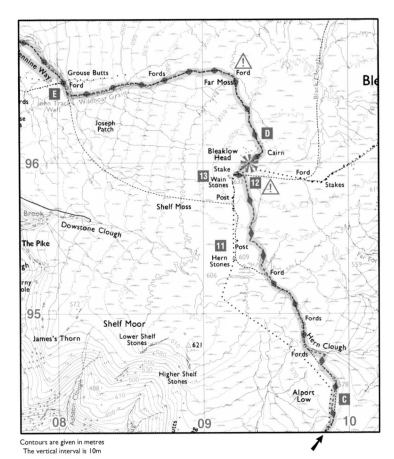

Contours are given in metres
The vertical interval is 10m

After a waymarker **C**, GPS 53° 26.941 01° 51.209, the route emerges on higher ground before bending left, north-west, to cross a stream at Hern Clough.

Follow the Clough, which becomes a waymarked channel, with some sections stone-slabbed. Just after crossing a stream, the Herne Stones **11**, GPS 53° 27.292 01° 51.750, can be seen on your left and are worth the short detour. Continue north, following waymarks, to a huge cairn – a pole and stones – marking the summit of **Bleaklow Head 12** (2,076 feet/633 metres), GPS 53° 27.678 01° 51.586.

From this bleak and spooky spot you can detour south-west to look for the curious Wain Stones **13** (which look like they're

kissing, remarked Wainwright) and the unsettling plane wreck, west.

Navigation from here can be tricky, as the path is rather vague. Head north **D**, following a waymarker and cairns, before turning left, north-west, then west, following a sunken, sandy path downhill. The Way continues to descend to where streams meet at John Track Well **E**, GPS 53° 27.882 01° 52.767.

From here route-finding is much easier and you relax and enjoy the fine moorland panoramas. A clear paved path heads north-west as it traces the beguiling cleft of Torside Clough, taking you gradually downhill towards the Torside Reservoir. Where the path finally meets a track, turn left and down to the road. Cross over, turn right, then left at a picnic spot 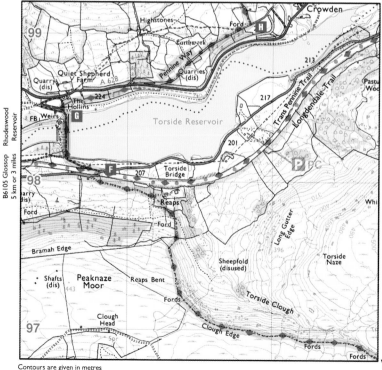. Cross the wall between the two reservoirs and turn right up a flight of steps. Go to the right of a white stile and walk through the pine plantation to the A628(T).

Cross the road to go right up a tarmac track and just beyond a plantation you meet a junction . If you're stopping in Crowden, go downhill to the campsite and youth hostel (through a gate on your left just after the campsite). If you're continuing on, take the left.

The first leg of any long-distance path is always tough and many days will be easier, including tomorrow. But for now give yourself a pat on the back and don't forget to have a good stretch.

Public transport

Edale (on route) ≋ 🚌 **Crowden** (on route) 🚌

Refreshments, public toilets and information

Edale (on route) 🍺 The Old Nags Head, The Rambler Country House ☕ Edale Cottage Café, Cooper's Café
Food shops: Edale
Public toilets: Edale
Information: Edale (The Moorland Centre), Edale Visitor Centre (01433 670207)

Accommodation

Edale (on route) wide selection
Upper Booth (on route) Upper Booth Farm (camping & barn)
Glossop (3 miles/4.8 km) The Old House (B&B, bunks), Windy Harbour Farm Hotel (B&B, camping), Avondale
Crowden (0.2 mile/0.3 km) Camping and Caravanning Clubsite, Crowden YHA

Contours are given in metres
The vertical interval is 10m

2 Crowden to Standedge

over Black Hill and across Wessenden Moor
11 miles (18 km)

Ascent 2,165 feet (660 metres)
Descent 1,575 feet (480 metres)
Highest point Black Hill: 1,908 feet (582 metres)
Lowest point Crowden: 656 feet (200 metres)

Are you ready for moor? Though it includes the notorious (for Wainwright at least) Black Hill, today is comparatively short and undemanding, mostly moorland walking and often on stone flagstones. Not as tough, or as scenic, as yesterday. But in the big skies, melancholy moorland vistas and some invitingly picturesque valleys, the walk has stacks of charm. Those who don't like reservoirs, however, are about to suffer (grr).

Route-finding is mostly straightforward, but Standedge has little in the way of facilities and you may want to think about kipping in nearby Diggle or Marsden. There are almost no options en route for stocking up, though if you're lucky there's a snack van on the A635.

Things to look out for

1 Laddow Rocks These rocks have been popular with Manchester climbers since the 'discovery' of the Pennines way back in 1901. First explored by E. A. Baker and others in that year, in 1916 Norwegian Ivar Berg bivvied in the cave to climb Cave Crack and Cave Arête. Wearing clogs. Indeed this was one of the first places in the country where rock climbing was practised.

Cottongrass Most of today's slopes are covered in cottongrass. In autumn they can be a beautiful orange and in early summer a pretty fluffy white. Common cottongrass has loose, dropping flowerheads of long silky hairs, with usually two or three heads on each stem. On drier ground look for hare's-tale common grass, which has single, more compact flowers. Getting to know your cottongrass could mean keeping your feet dry.

3 Black Hill Even more than Bleaklow, Black Hill suffers from notoriety. 'Every hill and every mountain is worth climbing,' said you-know-who, in *Wainwright on the Pennine Way*, 'the only exception being Black Hill.' After a 'gruelling trek through glutinous slime,' the crabby wanderer got stuck in a bog up here in an incident he called the 'most frightening experience of my long life'. 'No other [hill] shows such a desolate and hopeless quagmire to the sky,' he said, even if he finally recognised a 'certain strange beauty'. Barry Hilton, too, called it 'the landscape of a nightmare moon', with 'bottomless black pools of evil liquid mud'. However, the hill's nightmare reputation is long gone and there's a good path now. The trig point is known as Soldiers' Lump, to commemorate the efforts of the Royal Engineers who surveyed the land here in the 19th century. Mountain hares have been seen around Black Hill (in their white winter coats even in June sometimes), while it's also worth keeping an eye out for Pennine foxes today.

■ **Last of the Summer Wine Country**
If inexplicable images of horny old men bombing down hillsides in bathtubs pop into your head as you walk down towards the picturesque Wessenden reservoir, there's no need to question your sanity. *Last of the Summer Wine*, the world's longest-running television comedy series (1973–2010), was filmed around here, specifically in nearby Holmfirth to the east. If you're a fan (and I've got a feeling you secretly are), in Holmfirth you can see Wrinkled Stocking Tea Rooms (just off the Huddersfield Road), the Nora Batty steps and a pair of Compo's wellies.

Laddow Rocks – where Norwegians climb in clogs.

4 **Standedge** Standedge is little more than a cutting in the hillside for the road to pass through, but the magic happens underground. Several hundred feet beneath you, rail and canal tunnels run for 3 miles (4.8 km) between the village of Diggle, Greater Manchester, and Marsden, West Yorkshire. Standedge Tunnel is the highest, longest and deepest canal tunnel in the UK and the canal took 17 years and the lives of 50 men to complete. The first engineer was sacked when it was realised the two ends of the tunnel were at different heights and so would not meet, and five reservoirs were constructed to feed it. The Standedge Tunnel Visitor Centre in Marsden is well worth a visit.

Today also takes you through Last of the Summer Wine country.

Route description

From Crowden the Way starts out through a field, then on a dry stony track, ascending as it heads north-north-west towards **Laddow Rocks 1**. The route tiptoes below Black Tor and, after a ford, Rake Rocks, as a sign warns of deep bogs (unhelpfully, in the direction you've just come from). It climbs among boulders and gets steeper to go across Oakenclough Brook **A**, GPS 53° 30.286 01° 54.776.

Make sure you glance back regularly for some wonderful views of the valley, the behemoth of Bareholme Moss **2** on your left and the Bleaklow tablelands behind you (you may find yourself shaking your fist and yelling 'Why I oughta . . . !').

The Way brings you to the top of a sandstone ridge and follows the cliff top (Laddow Rocks look more characterful looking back). Ignore a path to the left by a cairn **B**, GPS 53° 30.504 01° 54.968, and continue north-north-east. The route crosses side-streams and descends gently, often on those treasured stone slabs. The mostly paved path follows Crowden Great Brook across some fords, where there's a chance of wet feet, until the river meets Meadowgrain Clough.

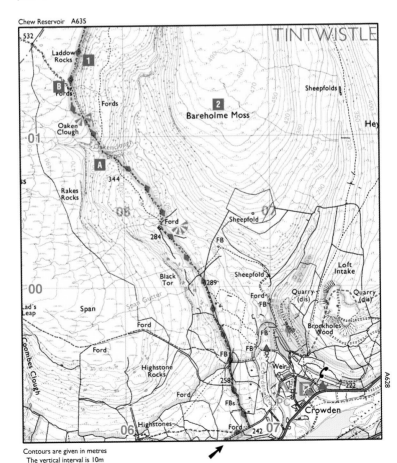

Contours are given in metres
The vertical interval is 10m

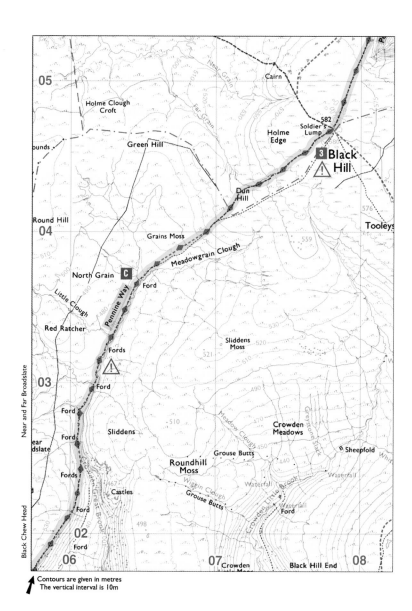

Contours are given in metres
The vertical interval is 10m

Leave the river behind and go over a stile **C**, GPS 53° 31.806 01° 54.218, for a straight ascent north-east over Dun Hill. Then, assuming you're feeling confident after your first victory of the day, head straight on – trying not to look too hard for hiker skeletons in the black bogs around you – to the triangulation column at the summit of **Black Hill** **3**, GPS 53° 32.328 01K 53.011.

In good weather, views open up in front of you (or so I'm told – I was smothered in fog) as you leave the plateau going north-west. You may see a large wind generator at Longley Farm near Holmfirth and, closer by, to the right, a 750-foot (229-metre) TV mast at Holme Moss (marking the nearest road to Black Hill, in case of a Wainwright-esque emergency). Head steeply downhill to a boundary ditch which, with the stone-slabbed path, forms a straight landmark heading directly towards the A635 road. If your luck's in (mine wasn't), Snoopy's snack van may be parked in a lay-by here.

Turn right and walk for a short distance on the road, then bear left along a side road for about 300 yards (275 metres)

towards Meltham and take the track to the left by the car park, leading on to Marsden Moor and down towards Wessenden Brook. This moor was once known as the Black Moor because it was bathed in soot from local mills and nearby industrial cities. But the habitat has long recovered and a meandering, gentle descent leads towards Wessenden Reservoir and an inviting panorama.

At the end of the Reservoir, take a left downhill (signposted Kirkless Way) and follow a wide track for about five minutes before a sharp left back downhill

The inviting descent towards Wessenden Reservoir (look out for randy old men in bathtubs).

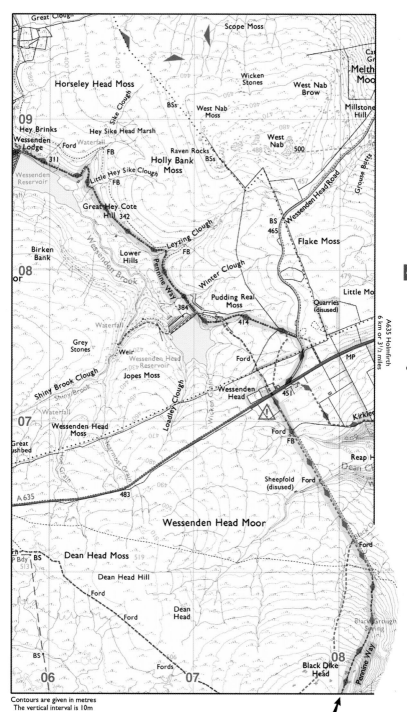

A635 Holmfirth
6 km or 3½ miles

Contours are given in metres
The vertical interval is 10m

(signposted) and across a stream , GPS 53° 34.642 01° 55.285. A short but steep climb takes you up the other side, then it's a gradual ascent along Blakely Clough.

At , GPS 53° 34.493 01° 56.562, bear right on a paved path leading to Black Moss Reservoir, with Great Butterly Hill rising like an orca to your right. This is another pretty stretch in the right weather, and even Wainwright grudgingly conceded it 'may even be described as enjoyable'.

Cross the reservoir along the wall and carry straight on, towards a fence and a heather-rich restoration area. At the fence turn left. When the restoration area ends (level with the end of the Black Moss Reservoir on your left), turn right

, GPS 53° 34.580 01° 57.288, on to a stone-slab pathway bearing north-west towards the A62. Turn left just after a ford on to a stony track, then you're at the road, and Standedge **4**. (If you're overnighting in Marsden, at the Great Western or the Carriage House, you may want to leave the way at the ford and head west, via the Redbrook Reservoir. Buses also run through Standedge to Diggle and Marsden, but you may need to wave them down.)

There's not much in Standedge, so a good alternative for accommodation is Diggle, to the west. It's not far off route and some places offer a lift to the welcoming Great Western for dinner, and a packed lunch for tomorrow.

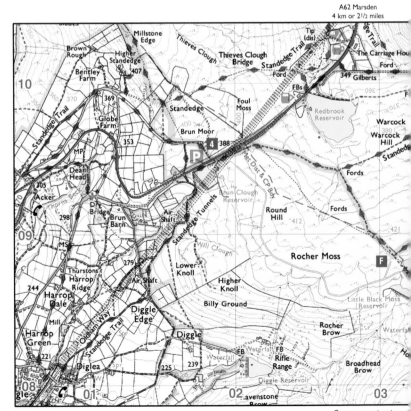

Contours are given in met
The vertical interval is 10

Public transport

Marsden (2 miles/3.2 km) ⇌
Standedge (on route) 🚌

Refreshments, public toilets and information

Standedge (on route) 🍺 The Great Western, Carriage House
Diggle (0.3 mile/0.5 km) 🍺 Diggle Hotel
Information: Marsden Tourist Information Centre (01484 845595, informationpoint@Kirklees.gov.uk)

Accommodation

Standedge (on route) Great Western (camping),
Carriage House (inc. camping)
Diggle (0.3 mile/0.5 km) Rock Farm, New Barn, Sunfield Accommodation
Marsden (2 miles/3.2 km) Tunnel End Inn
Delph (0.6 mile/1 km) Wellcroft House

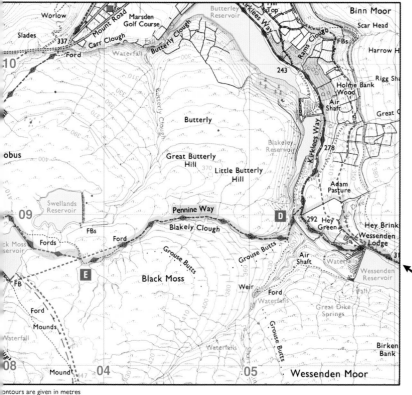

contours are given in metres
The vertical interval is 10m

3 Standedge to Calder Valley

via Blackstone Edge, reservoirs and Stoodley Pike
11 miles (18 km)

Ascent 1,150 feet (350 metres)

Descent 2,100 feet (640 metres)

Highest point Blackstone Edge: 1,549 feet (472 metres)

Lowest point Callis Bridge: 590 feet (180 metres)

'The worst part of the journey is behind you,' says Wainwright, 'from now on the Pennine Way can be enjoyed.' In truth, however, today probably isn't one that will linger long in the memory. This stretch lacks the scenic splendour of the last two days and the sounds of 'civilisation' (i.e. the niggling buzz of traffic) are never far away. However, there's still much to enjoy, especially the views approaching Calder Valley, under the watchful eye of Stoodley Pike, which dominates the second half of the day.

There's plenty of flat walking and much of this section sticks to high moors and gritstone edges. By teatime, however, some will be pig sick of all the reservoirs.

Navigation is potentially tricky only along Blackstone Edge in foul weather, but there are cairns and poles to guide you.

Unusually, today there are some tempting lunchtime refreshment options, a pub and (probably) a snack van.

Hebden Bridge has good accommodation options but is 1 mile (1.6 km) off route. Blackshaw Head, Jack Bridge or even Colden are alternatives, which add a bit on to today but mean starting the next day from the top of a torturous hill. Staying in Todmorden (Mankinholes) would make it a shorter day.

Things to look out for

5 Blackstone Edge Pioneering female traveller Celia Fiennes toured Britain on horseback in the late 17th century, keeping a diary of her adventures. She described how Blackstone Edge was 'noted all over England for [being] a dismal high precipice'. She called it 'very troublesome' and noted its 'formidableness'. She lamented the moist ground, 'a sort of a mist', the perpetual rain and compared the area to the Italian Alps. You sense she wouldn't have enjoyed the Pennine Way very much. *Robinson Crusoe* author Daniel Defoe labelled the Edge a 'fearful precipice'

and, getting a little carried away, compared it to the Andes. The scenery changes here from the peat moorlands, marshes and groughs to a greener, friendlier landscape. Or as Wainwright put it: 'Life comes good again on Blackstone Edge.' After here the Way leaves the watershed and isn't reunited with it until Pen-y-ghent.

6 Roman Road This ancient trans-Pennine route is marked on maps as a Roman road. In places the cobbled and flagged stones are impressively preserved, but like most things its origins are open to debate. It could have been built in the 18th century – probably following a much older route. You can see a central groove, which is more common with the construction of packhorse routes. Some historians believe the groove was used for drainage, others that it aided vehicles braking on the steep incline.

6 Aiggin Stone The Stone is likely to have been connected to the Roman road, possibly as a medieval waymarker to guide folk across the duplicitous Blackstone Ridge. As with the road, its exact origins are frustratingly obscure but it's thought to be around 600 years old.

Reservoirs By the end of the day, a diligent fellow Wayfarer informed me, you will have passed 14 reservoirs so far on the Way. Clearly some people think it rains a lot around here. Several of the water basins, including Blackstone Edge, Chelburn, Light Hazzles, White Holme and Warland, were built to provide for the Rochdale Canal, which opened in 1804. Nowadays the water from here goes into the kettles of Oldham and Rochdale. Walkers may be divided on whether they're an eyesore or photograph-worthy. I hate them. They're almost always accompanied by a flat, stony path that saps energy, hurts feet and makes otherwise tough guidebook writers want to cry.

8 Stoodley Pike Calder Valley has had a tower or pike watching over it from a hilltop since the early 18th century, but the defeat of Napoleon in 1814 prompted the erection of a new monument, to peace. Annoyingly, the French warmonger escaped from exile on the island of Elba in 1815, so work on the project was postponed (boo). Napoleon, however, met his Waterloo at, er, the Battle of Waterloo and work was completed (yay). Only for the construction to collapse in 1854 after a lightning strike (boo). Two years later another, lightning-proof, monument replaced it (yay) and still stands today at 125 feet (38 metres). For better or worse, it will dominate the walk for half of today and tomorrow.

10 Hebden Bridge This town is a child of the Industrial Revolution. Once little more than an inn and a bridge, the 19th century brought water power, the railway and a string of cotton mills to make it an international centre for the fustian trade (a type of cotton cloth). Foreign competition killed it off, but you can still find soot on walls from its heyday, plus old mills and double-decker terraces. Hebden has ample facilities (shops, ATMs, a post office, heck, even a cinema – imagine!), which may excite some Wayfarers and repel others. It's a culture shock after blissful days of meditative moorland and modest villages, but Hebden is very likeable. It's known for its 'alternative crowd', which as usual means great cafés and folk music in pubs. Even Wainwright conceded it had charm, likening the hillside terraces to Tibetan monasteries. He recommended a rest day here to visit 'one of the most renowned beauty spots in the north of England', Hardcastle Crags. To get there, follow Hebden Water on a woodland walk of 'bewitching beauty'.

Standedge to Calder Valley

Calder Valley and towers have an eventful history, thanks in no small part to an irksome French warmonger (and the odd bit of lightning).

Route description

From the car park **A**, cross the A62 – leaving the Peak District – and follow a sandy track. Bear left for 100 yards (90 metres) and straight ahead at a junction. After another 100 yards (90 metres) bear right through a narrow gate by a signpost (ignoring the sign for the Pennine Bridleway). Continue through gates and along a well-worn path up to Standedge ridge. Then north-west, following occasional cairns and poles, to the triangulation point **B**, GPS °53 35.420 01° 58.966, at the zenith of Millstone Edge.

Views from here show one of the most densely populated landscapes in Europe – Rochdale, Oldham, Bury, Bolton, Greater Manchester – so for once I was grateful for thick fog, making it feel I was many miles from the world of brick and tarmac. Along here, huge boulders have contorted into all sorts of eccentric shapes.

The route clings to the gritstone edge, with some cairns, passing the Ammon Wrigley Memorial Stone (local poet/writer/character) and the Dinner Stone. Go across several shallow cloughs then turn right, north-east, by a stone waymarker, GPS 53° 35.866 01° 59.680, towards the crest of a hill. Above Blea Green the Way turns away from the edge on a path north, then north-west, by Oldgate Moss to the smaller dome of Little Moss **1**. Descend to meet the A640 **C**.

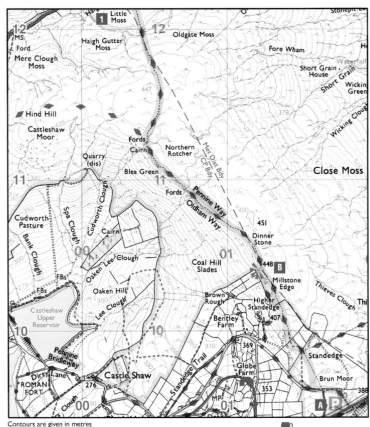

Contours are given in metres
The contour values are 5m and 10m

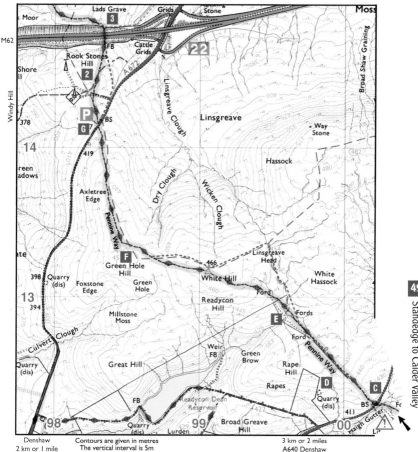

Denshaw
2 km or 1 mile

Contours are given in metres
The vertical interval is 5m

3 km or 2 miles
A640 Denshaw

Over the road go north-west uphill, on an old packhorse route, aiming for what looks like a rock outcrop or cairns on the skyline, though it's actually the end of a wall **D**, GPS 53° 36.523 02° 00.051. Continue beside it, then drop down to cross over a shallow clough **E**, GPS 53° 36.749 02° 00.448, where Readycon Dean Reservoir can be seen to the left, before rising again to the brow of White Hill, suitably decorated with a white triangulation point, GPS 53° 36.910 02° 00.934.

Wainwright suggested the next stretch would have walkers questioning their sanity, but he must have been cursed with bad weather again, because it was pleasant enough for me. The Way veers north-north-west on a good clear path **F**, below the northern slopes of Green Hole Hill. Descend along Axletree Edge with the radio mast of Windy Hill and the M62 directly ahead. Cross the A672, an old turnpike road, at a lay-by **G**, GPS 53° 37.434 02° 01.625, where hopefully there's a snack van parked.

Continue north, into West Yorkshire, passing to the right of a massive Windy Mill mast **2**, and on a track on the right, down along a stony then stone-slabbed path, to the M62, where a footbridge **3** takes you safely over the M62.

After the bridge take a path to the left, which soon veers right, north-west.

Follow a stony track up towards Blackstone Edge, with Green Withens Reservoir seen down on your right. The path gets vague – look for cairns and poles – and some boulder-hopping may be required and is good fun.

The triangulation point 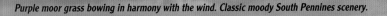, GPS 53° 38.636 02° 02.618, stands on Blackstone Edge 5, a broad whaleback of rock at 1,549 feet (472 metres), today's highest point. There are, apparently, good views west and east and you may even be able to pick out Stoodley Pike to the north (or so I'm told – I was still battling with the fog monster).

Leaving the crest ridge, path-finding can be tricky. Pick your way between giant gritstone boulders, looking for cairns and poles, as the path descends a little, before undulating through more boulders. Eventually you go through a kissing-gate and on to a track, where you'll instantly find the Aiggin Stone 6, GPS °53 39.008 02° 02.511. For the next 3 miles (4.8 km) the Way spends its only time wholly in Lancashire.

Follow the track left, west, and downhill as the stones evolve into the paved 'Roman road', once nicknamed the Devil's Pavement. Cross the small footbridge over Broad Head Drain and turn right, north H, GPS 53° 38.968 02° 02.855, along a 6-foot (2-metre)-wide track. Follow this to a fork and turn downhill to the left, west, towards the A58 and the inviting site of the White House Inn 7. There are very few opportunities for pub lunches or afternoon ales along the Way, so you might want to take advantage. I didn't, and I regretted it at lunchtime every day afterwards for the rest of the trail.

Wainwright thought the next stretch the easiest of the whole Way (I thought it a P in the A). Turn right at the road after crossing it and left along a track by the Blackstone Edge Reservoir. The grassy bank below the dam wall can be dotted with eyebright and clover. At the end of the reservoir stick to the wide sandy track and follow another spillway called Head Drain.

The going is flat here and for a while there are pretty views down to the left, into Light Hazzles Clough. You may see purple moor grass (Molinia) here, which looks mauve or purple from a distance in summer but otherwise a tasteful yellow, and Canada geese. As the name suggests, they're not native, but there are certainly worse types of introduced species.

Purple moor grass bowing in harmony with the wind. Classic moody South Pennines scenery.

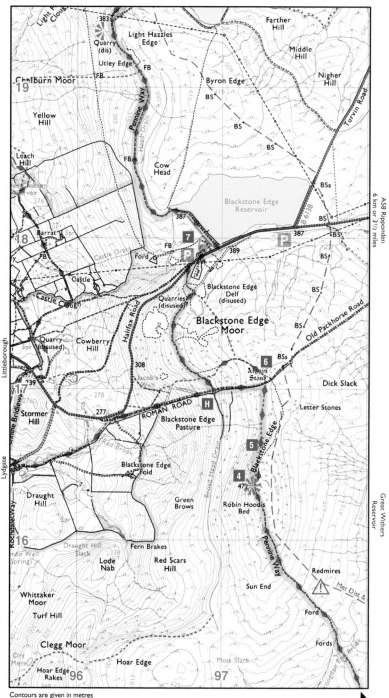

Contours are given in metres
The vertical interval is 5m

Onwards and upwards past a solitary standing stone and towards Stoodley Pike.

The Way continues along the track under the unsettling electricity pylons (not right, along the waymarked Reservoir Circuit) and beside Light Hazzles Reservoir. At the reservoir's end, GPS 53° 40.788 02° 03.628, stay on the upper path alongside the Warland Reservoir. At that reservoir's end you return to the moorland, following the Warland Drain and flagstones, with the Holder Stone visible to the south-east, and you'll soon see Stoodley Pike rising proudly, almost menacingly, in the distance – not unlike Isengard in *The Lord of the Rings*.

Hopefully it's not too much of a drain (guffaw) sticking with the drain as it doglegs right. When the drain turns sharp right ▮, GPS 53° 41.668 02° 03.323, leave it and continue north on a stone-slabbed path over Langfield Common, heading slightly to the right of the rock-scattered summit of Coldwell Hill. At a cairn there are cracking views all around, but you're heading north-east towards Stoodley Pike, the hill-top needle which never seems to get any closer. Views of the tree-lined Calder Valley below start to reveal themselves. It's a pretty sight, even if the straight lines of walls and fields can be a small shock to the system after all that wonderfully amorphous moorland.

At the bottom of the hill the Way crosses the Caldervale Way at Withens Gate ▮, GPS 53° 42.279 02° 03.092, where there are several paths trying to lead you astray (though going downhill to Mankinholes youth hostel is a possible overnight option).

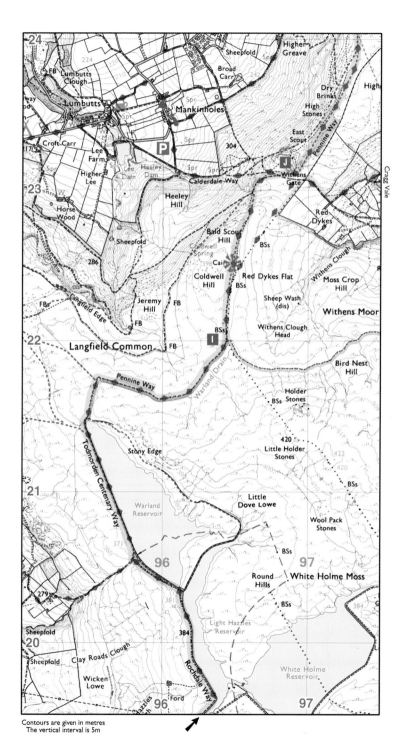

Contours are given in metres
The vertical interval is 5m

Head on, following some cairns and the hill crest of Higher Moor, to **Stoodley Pike** 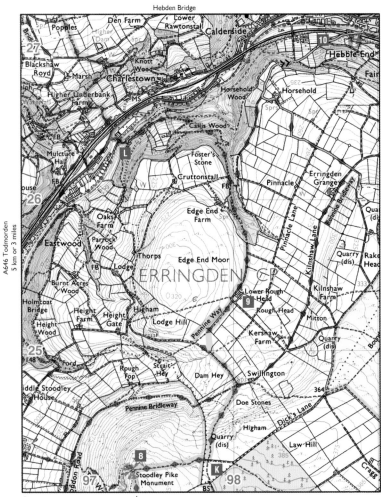, GPS 53° 42.861 02° 02.545. You can climb its dark (grab your torch) spiralling staircase for even better views of a valley that, from here, hides its industrial heritage behind a veil of amiable greenery.

Head east, down a clear, wide path towards a plantation, through a stile in a wall. Turn left through a gate **K**, GPS 53° 42.899 02° 02.067, to go steeply

downhill. Take a slight left to carry on downhill by a wall. Go right over a stile and across a field on flagstones. After a gate follow the wall and head towards Lower Rough Head Farm **9**, GPS °53 43.488 °02 01.903. Kink left on to a track and carry on north, to the left of the farm.

Follow the track through pretty Callis Wood, thriving with alder, birch, willow and a few oak and wych-elms. In early summer you might see March thistle,

Standedge to Calder Valley

A646 Todmorden 5 km or 3 miles

Hebden Bridge

Contours are given in metres
The vertical interval is 5m

Wainwright likened the hillside terraces of Hebden Bridge to Tibetan monasteries. He never went to Asia, but it's a decent shout all the same.

celery-leaved buttercup, rosebay, meadowsweet, hemlock water-dropwart, plus foxgloves and bluebells.

After a signposted shortcut through the woods continue west along the track. Soon you'll see colourful barges and the canal, right next to train tracks and a road, looking like a display in some kind of history of transport museum. Turn right **L**, GPS 53°44.035 02° 02.607, to cross the Rochdale Canal and the River Calder.

If you're staying in Hebden Bridge **10**, head right, east, along the towpath, or road, into town (real-ale fans will enjoy the folky Fox and Goose Inn).

The Calder Valley is the first time down from the gritstone plateaux since Crowden and it marks a definitive stage of the Way. The bleak peat moors are behind you and green pastoral scenery takes over. Of course, such terrain means it's more civilised, for better or worse.

Public transport

Blackstone Edge (A58, on route)
Todmorden (2 miles/3.2 km)
Hebden Bridge (1 mile/1.6 km)

Refreshments, public toilets and information

A672 (on route) snack van
Blackstone Edge (on route) White House
Hebden Bridge (1 mile/1.6 km) wide selection
Mankinholes (1 mile/1.6 km) Shepherd's Rest Inn
Food shops: Hebden Bridge, Colden
Public toilets: Hebden Bridge
Information: Hebden Bridge (Tourist

Information Centre, 01422 843831, www.hebdenbridge.co.uk), Todmorden (Tourist Information Centre, 01706 818181, www.visittodmorden.co.uk)

Accommodation

Todmorden (1.5 mile/2.4 km) Towneley Trail Bed and Box, Mankinholes YHA, Cross Farm
Hebden Bridge (1 mile/1.6 km) wide selection
Blackshaw Head (0.1 mile/0.2 km) Badger Fields Farm
Colden (0.1 mile/0.2 km) Highgate Farm
Jack Bridge (0.5 mile/0.8 km) New Delight Inn

4 Calder Valley to Ickornshaw

via Heptonstall Moor, Brontë country and Ickornshaw Moor
16 miles (26 km)

Ascent 2,885 feet (880 metres)

Descent 2,490 feet (760 metres)

Highest point Withins Height: 1,472 feet (449 metres)

Lowest point Callis Bridge: 590 feet (180 metres)

Though there are a few potential route-finding blind spots, today is relatively undemanding and yet attractive. There's all the Brontë stuff to enjoy too of course, and maybe it's the literary associations or maybe it's the moors themselves (which came first, etc?), but some of today's landscapes do seem especially dreamy and ruminative. That said, it starts with a cruel climb out of the Calder Valley, even if in spring it's through joyful pastures full of loony lambs leaping about. There's a beautiful stretch over wind-whispering, mellow yellow Heptonstall Moor, to the literary landscapes of Brontë country and up again on to bleaker Ickornshaw Moor. Naturally there are some reservoirs too (groan).

Route-finding could be testing on both moors in unfriendly conditions. Likewise, the twists and turns climbing up the Calder Valley need close attention.

For facilities, there's a legendary little shop and a pub en route, as well as Haworth, a little off route, but where some may chose to stay overnight as it has a good range of facilities. Cowling and neighbouring Ickornshaw don't have many accommodation options, so if you're heading there book ahead.

Things to look out for

■ **Brontë country** The Brontës were one of the most remarkable literary families in English literature, with three of the six children becoming writers, two of them ranking amongst the greatest novelists of the 19th century. They grew up in Haworth in the early 1800s. After their mother died and their father succumbed to alcoholism, an austere aunt looked after the six children. Four of them would die from tuberculosis, but not before Emily's *Wuthering Heights*, Anne's *Agnes Grey* and Charlotte's *Jane Eyre* were all published in 1847. Charlotte was the only one to have any sort of real literary success in her lifetime. However, she struggled with loneliness and frustration, before dying in pregnancy. Of all the Brontës' novels, it's in *Wuthering Heights* that the moors most vividly come to life, their wild, moody presence and forceful weather mirroring the brooding character of Heathcliff. Top Withins, which the Way passes, has become a pilgrimage site for *Wuthering Heights* fans. A Brontë

Society plaque on the ruin says that although the former farmhouse has been associated with the Earnshaw home in the novel, it 'bore no resemblance to the house she described'. However, 'the situation may have been in her mind when she wrote [it]'. There's less disputing that characterful 17th-century farmhouse Ponden Hall was the inspiration for Thrushcross Grange.

Haworth The Way doesn't pass through Haworth, but some will want to detour there, via the Brontë Bridge and Brontë Falls. You can also peer in on the Brontë's former home, now the Brontë Parsonage Museum, and the Black Bull where the only Brontë brother, Branwell, over-indulged. Aside from its literary attractions, Wainwright thought the village 'should certainly be visited once in a lifetime'. As well as its signature steep, cobbled streets and gritstone buildings, there are lots of accommodation and eating options and other facilities for us walkers. Bear in mind Haworth can be chocka with tourists in summer.

7 8 Ickornshaw and Cowling

Cowling may be recorded in the Domesday book, but it isn't the prettiest place you'll stay on the Way. However, it has a couple of accommodation options, surprisingly good food on offer (the Indian restaurant comes recommended), a post office/shop and an average pub. Neighbouring Ickornshaw, pretty much an extension of Cowling, has a more attractive aura, though facilities are pretty limited.

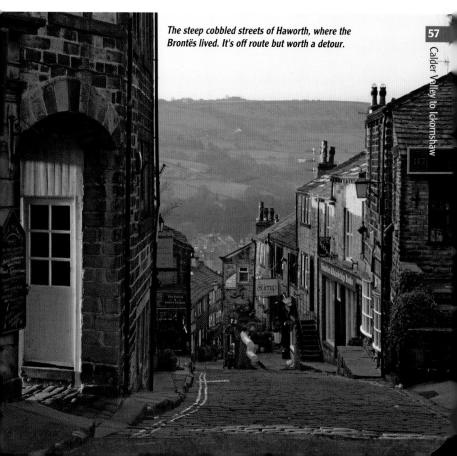

The steep cobbled streets of Haworth, where the Brontës lived. It's off route but worth a detour.

Route description

You'll need to be alert this morning, as the start is a little complicated. Cross the busy A646 just to the west of Hebden Bridge 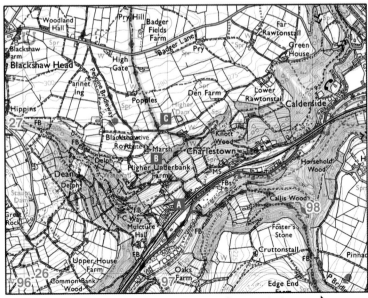, turning right then left into Underbank Avenue. After about 100 yards go under a bridge and up a very steep, cobbled path. Turn left on a track and follow it through Higher Underbank Farm. Looking back, Stoodley Pike is still watching you from the distance.

Go past a derelict building and, after a ruined chapel and little graveyard, turn sharp right ■, GPS 53° 44.139 02° 02.958. Here you can follow the official Way, or take Wainwright's preferred route, by a marker. The former continues steadily uphill, to turn left on to the road, left again at some buildings then, after 100 yards, right through a gap in a wall on to a grassy path ■, GPS 53° 44.338 02° 02.881. Continue north over more fields until you cross a road (Badger Fields Farm, a B&B and campsite, is on your right).

Meanly, the path starts to descend again, into Colden Valley, on a very narrow path

between two walls. Cross a beautiful heather-lined track (the New Delight Inn, which has accommodation, is west of here in Jack Bridge) with widening views of the Colden Clough and Heptonstall Church, where poet Sylvia Plath is buried.

Go down a steep bank of heather and bilberry, aiming for an old packhorse bridge at Hebble Hole ■, GPS 53° 45.014 02° 03.029. It carries both the Pennine Way and the Calderdale Way over the water at an enchanting spot where dippers and grey wagtails live.

Ignore the slabbed Calderdale Way to the right and climb steeply uphill, bearing left around Goose Head Farm and north again to meet the Burnley–Hebden Bridge road ■, GPS 53° 45.254 02° 03.160. A little further on you reach a smaller side road. About 250 yards off route to your left lies the legendary if extravagantly titled May's Aladdin's Cave Highgate Farm Shop (which also has free camping). It's very friendly and, from jelly babies to plasters, has all the supplies you could wish for.

Contours are given in metres
The vertical interval is 5m

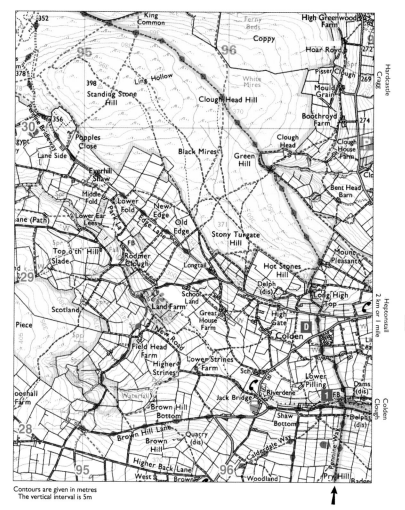

Contours are given in metres
The vertical interval is 5m

Otherwise, cross the road with a slight kink to the right and head straight up to cross a brow. From the farm buildings, descend diagonally left across the moor, heading approximately for the walled corner of a field on the shoulder of Hot Stones Hill, aiming to put the derelict if poetic-looking farmhouse on your right.

The path ahead, which is flagged in places, veers gradually left, north-west, up Clough Head Hill and into a dreamy expanse of yellow moorland, with, finally, no man-made shapes to be seen. It felt liberating

to be back on the moors after and the next hour was my favourite part of the day.

It could be tricky around here in bad weather, so look for a Pennine Way signpost, GPS 53° 46.078 02° 03.763, and carry on north-west at a crossroads. As the path slowly starts to descend there are almost no landmarks to guide you, so keep the dome of Standing Stone Hill to your left. As the path improves, you'll soon spy possibly the loneliest-looking pub you've ever seen (at least until the Tan Hill Inn): the Pack Horse Inn.

Follow a fence and wall down towards Gorple Lower Reservoir (ugh). Turn right down a track and through a gate to Gorple Cottages. Cross straight over the road and continue downhill into a beautiful rocky hollow **E**, GPS 53° 46.788 02° 04.824. After crossing two footbridges go left and continue above Graining Water, through a gate, up a slabbed track and alongside a wall. Go right at the first stile for the Pack Horse Inn; or keep going until a right between two walls brings you to the road.

Ignore the step-stile to the right, turn left and pass Well Hole Cottage. Turn right near a lay-by **F**, up the grass bank and on to a tarmac track towards the Gorple reservoirs. Take the (signposted) third right turn, towards the dam wall of Walshaw Dean

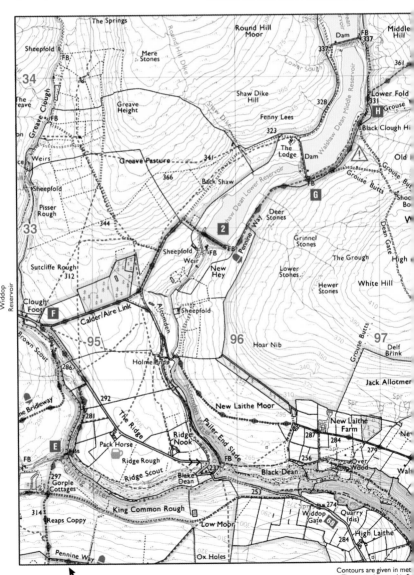

Contours are given in met
The vertical interval is 5r

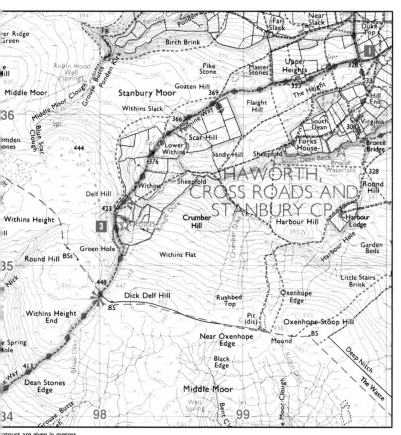

Contours are given in metres
The vertical interval is 5m

Lower reservoir **2**. Cross the dam wall and turn left to follow a path above the reservoir shore. You may see Canada geese, pied wagtail and mallard. Pass the dam wall (all these damn walls!) of the middle of the reservoir **G** along a path between the concrete spillway and the water.

The path turns left **H** over a walled bridge and through a gate, then right, uphill along a stone-slabbed path to the brow of a hill. You can now see all three reservoirs – *and* Stoodley Pike. Will that irksome monument be forever in your rear-view mirror?

Ahead and to the left is a broken spine of a wall leading to the ruins of Top Withins **3**, GPS 53° 48.893 02° 01.776, where a few Brontë fans may be loitering, looking

slightly disappointed. But there's no denying the romance and remoteness of the wind-whipped place. Wainwright, of course, hated it, complaining it was 'harsh and sour, without life and without beauty'. But I'd happily live here (if it wasn't for tourists and those pesky Pennine Wayfarers).

The Way drops downhill, passing levelled ruins (more Withins). Follow the track, eventually bearing east-north-east past Upper Heights Farm (with a date-mark of 1761 and a mysterious face above the door; accommodation is available). Below, bear left when the track forks and pass Lower Heights Farm. Turn left off the track **I**, GPS 53° 49.422 02° 00.269, to join the Brontë Way literary trail on a grassy track heading down from the moor.

Veer right **J** to Buckley Green (with another date-mark), then switchback left on the track at the bottom, towards Buckley House. Just before the house bear right over a stile, down a sunken path. Continue through pastures, past a derelict barn and a farm. From the road you can either go right to **Howarth** (2.5 mile/ 4 km), or left on the Pennine Way.

The Way follows the private road beside the reservoir and up to Ponden Hall **4** (nearby Ponden House has

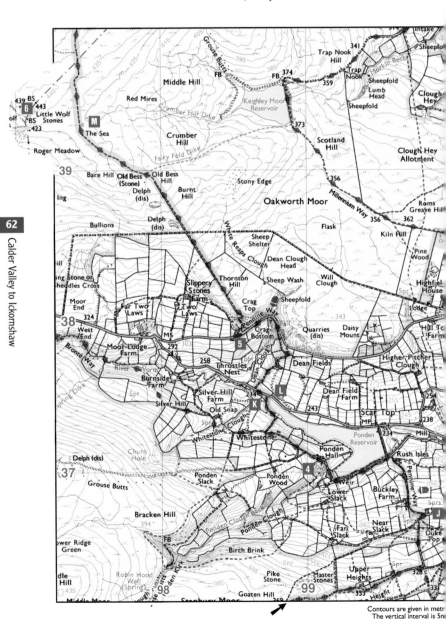

Contours are given in metr
The vertical interval is 5n

While the association between Top Withins and Wuthering Heights is dubious, Ponden Hall's connection to Emily Brontë's Thrushcross Grange is more obvious. Yet you'll find fewer tourists here.

accommodation). Follow the track past the outbuildings and high above the reservoir. Tarmac becomes grass by a gate, then the route descends. Take a sharp right over the bridge at the head of the reservoir , GPS 53° 50.013 02° 01.260, and on to the Colne–Howarth road .

Turn left along the road, briefly, while mentally preparing for a testing little climb. Cross a stone step-stile and head directly uphill on a steep grassy path, sticking close to the wall. Follow the path through a gap in the wall to the right, above the house and over pastureland (Dean Fields).

Pass to the right of a ruined barn, bear left along a track and over a stile, then on past a house to the right and along a walled track. Go past a set of old gateposts and turn sharp left, off the farm track, then follow an old wall-line to a step-stile. Walk by a wall with a wood on the left until you reach a road. The small woodland is blessed with (pink) American willowherb and buckler ferns.

Turn left to go over Crag Bottom at the head of Dean Clough. Cross a bridge and continue to Crag Bottom Farm **5**, GPS 53° 50.238 02° 01.462 (look for its mullioned windows). Turn right, off the road here, climbing to Crag Top, which bequeaths some cracking views.

North towards Thornton Hill, the route goes over a fence-stile, with a wall on the left. You're back on the moor and vegetation quickly changes costume to the more familiar bilberry and swathes of rushes, hinting at marshy ground. Follow the fence, or fence and wall, until Old Bess Hill.

The path bears slightly left, uphill over open moorland which Wainwright labelled 'a barren wasteland', but again, in half-decent weather, with those big, big skies full of more drama than a cinema screen, I enjoyed this stretch. As it levels off on to a wide hill crest, appropriately called The Sea **M**, you should see the triangulation pillar at the Wolf Stones ahead **6**. Bear right, GPS 53° 50.999 02° 02.460, before the pillar and follow the path, which is slabbed intermittently.

You're now on Ickornshaw Moor, enjoyed by grouse, curlew and golden plover, but not by you if you get lost. With few landmarks, the next section could be tricky in unsympathetic conditions.

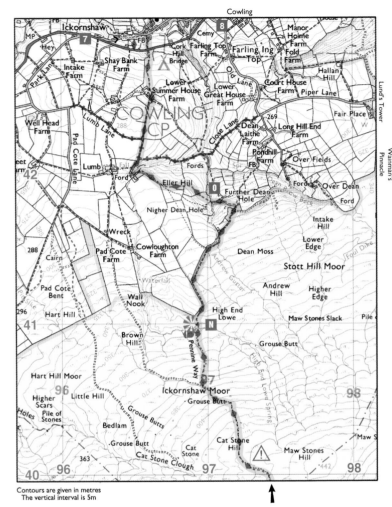

Cowling

Contours are given in metres
The vertical interval is 5m

The path weaves north and north-west past a wooden pole and a small stone wind shelter, GPS 53° 51.470 02° 02.544. Slabs are intermittent again, as are cairns, and in good weather you'll be able aim for the stone hut , GPS 53° 51.911 02° 02.905, to the north, as the often sunken and sandy path descends towards it.

Pen-y-ghent, which will have you hot, sweaty and cursing in a day or two, can soon be seen up ahead. As can a sea of green hills so shapely and buxom they may well have some walkers missing their lady folk back home. To the right you should be able to see two monuments, Wainman's Pinnacle and Lund's Tower (locally nicknamed the salt and pepper pots); the former is another monument to the end of the Napoleonic Wars.

From the hut, the Way continues north over the brow of a hill and down a clear path beside a wall and past several huts. Bear sharp left after a wall-stile and downhill again, still beside a drystone wall on a grassy path.

Around here, approaching the urban world again, I got my usual late-afternoon sense of ambivalence about swapping moors for streets and heather for tarmac. Sure, I want a shower, but do I want the noises and smells of towns?

At the end of the wall continue downhill, following signposts to a gate. The path bears sharp left beside a wall and down past an abandoned farm to cross a stream (Andrew Gutter) at a footbridge **0** , GPS 53° 52.342 02° 02.798.

After a footbridge, skirt Eller Hill and circle above the waterfall at Lumb Head. Continue on a walled track, straight on rather than left along the more gravelled track at Lumb Lane. Then down, past

Lower Summer House, a small farm with a big noise coming from a chaotic collection of animals.

Over a stile in a wall, head north down a track, then over another wall and down through pasture, sticking loosely to the left. At the A6068 turn left, then after 60 yards (55 metres) cross the road with care and turn right by a Pennine Way signpost.

Go down the narrow path and turn right on to a smaller road. The Way continues on the first left, but if you're staying in Ickornshaw **7** (which you're now in) or Cowling **8** , carry straight on.

Public transport
Haworth (2.5 miles/4 km) 🚆 🚌
Cowling (0.3/0.4.8 km) 🚌

Refreshments, public toilets and information
Widdop (100 yards/90 metres) 🍴
Pack Horse Inn
Haworth (2.5 miles/4 km), wide selection; ATM in the Spar
Cowling (0.3/0.5 km) 🍴 The Dog & Gun
Food shops: Blackshaw Head (Highgate

Farm shop), Haworth, Cowling
Information: Haworth (Tourist Information, 01535 642329, haworth@ytbtic.co.uk)

Accommodation
Widdop (100 yards/90 metres) Packhorse Inn
Ponden (on route) Upper Heights Farm, Ponden House
Stanbury (0.3 mile/0.5 km) Old Silent Inn
Haworth (2.5 miles/4 km) wide selection
Ickornshaw (on route) Winterhouse Barn
Cowling (0.3/0.5 km) Woodland House

It's all the rage for valleys round here to have a tower – Lund's Tower also commemorates the end of the Napoleonic Wars.

5 Ickornshaw to Malham

via the Aire Gap, Thornton-in-Craven and Gargrave
17 miles (27 km)

Ascent 2,360 feet (719 metres)
Descent 1,970 feet (600 metres)
Highest point Pinhaw Beacon: 1,273 feet (388 metres)
Lowest point Gargrave: 351 feet (107 metres)

'Mostly muck and manure' is how the ever-joyful Wainwright described the first part of this section. Today probably won't rank in many people's Pennine Way Top 10, but there's a pot of gold at its end: Malham and the dramatic start of Limestone Country. 'Malham's the place where the highlights start to appear,' wrote Wainwright.

You're also saying hello – and, more enjoyably, goodbye – to the Aire Gap, the lowlands which form a geographical corridor between the South Pennines and Yorkshire Dales, or between millstone grit moors and limestone. The Romans built a road through it, but Bronze Age traders had long since used the route to travel between Ireland and Scandinavia. Elsewhere it's rolling pastures and flat riverside walking. Barge and bridge fans may love the section along the Leeds and Liverpool Canal, while there are fine views from Pinhaw Beacon and Scalaber Hill.

The Way passes through an unusual number of villages, meaning lots of facilities, including a couple of top-notch cafés and the chance to carry a lighter pack.

With all the villages and zigzagging through undulating fields where the path can be vague, it's a fiddly day for path-finding and you might want to keep this humble little guidebook of yours close to hand.

This stage could easily be shortened a little, by stopping in Gargrave, or a lot, by staying in just-off-route Earby.

Things to look out for

1 Lothersdale You can't mention Lothersdale, the last Pennine mill town as you go north, without reference to its incongruous chimney, which feels like a step back in time. The largest waterwheel in England is here, too, in the Dale End Mill. The charming village is also a centre of Quakerism, and the nearby mansion of Stone Gappe was the influence for Gateshead Hall in *Jane Eyre*. Wainwright calls Lothersdale 'a sweet and friendly village' and I too found myself sharing a joke with a local dog-walker. From here the landscape starts to change as it approaches the Aire Gap.

5 Leeds and Liverpool Canal Like many canals, its active life was brief but busy. In the 19th century it was a teeming highway for shortboats, narrowboats and packetboats, all towed by big, strong horses. The canal is 127 miles (204 km) long, with nine locks and a mile-long

(0.6-km) tunnel. But by the 1920s, the railway was the winner and the heyday of canals was over. The waterway has had a new lease of life recently as a leisure option and it's apparently better looking now than it ever was.

9 Malham Bill Bryson, author of *Notes From A Small Island* and many more hilarious travelogues, is a former Dales resident and a big Malham fan: 'I won't know for sure if Malhamdale is the finest place there is until I have died and seen heaven (assuming they let me at least have a glance), but until that day comes it will certainly do.' At the beginning of the last century Malham was known for mines and mills, but now it relies on tourism. And for good reason. It's in a gorgeous setting, with the limestone plateau reaching up behind it like a tsunami. Plus it's blessed with two items of glorious natural architecture nearby, in the Gordale Scar and Malham Cove. It is, however, one of the busiest villages in the Dales.

Gordale Scar No matter how knackered you are, this is an essential detour (drop your bag off first if you can). Wainwright thought the 'limestone magic' of the Scar more impressive than Malham Cove (which you'll see tomorrow morning), and the Tate Gallery has an atmospheric James Ward painting of the Scar from 1812. The dramatic slash in the limestone plateau, part of the Mid Craven Fault (a crack across the Pennines), looks like something left over from a Norse legend involving some implacably angry gods. You can climb up inside by the waterfall on to the limestone plateau for some very rewarding views back south. The best way to reach the Scar is via the slightly longer scenic route, the Janet's Foss walk (signposted from the Way just before Malham), which includes an alluring waterfall in an intimate little wooded cove (*foss* is Old Norse for falls). There's a popular campsite at the foot of the Scar.

The Gordale Scar (off route) gets less attention than Malham Cove but to many it's more impressive. Artist James Ward evidently thought so too – this is his dramatic painting.

Route description

From Ickornshaw, start up the metalled track (the first left, just after you turned right into Ickornshaw), past houses and along the edge of a field. Pass the edge of a row of terraced houses, following a wall beside a meadow. Turn right, through the wall, to a road. Go left along the road, bear right where the road forks and go downhill to Gill Bridge.

Cross the bridge and turn left, then, before a house, go right, along a track. After a stile, turn sharp right and uphill through meadowland, initially following a grassy path beside a pleasant stream decorated with watercress, lady's-smock, brooklime, plus bluebells in spring and early summer.

For the next 1.25 miles (2 km) the route goes through farmland between Low Stubbing and the derelict High Stubbing. Where the path meets a road **A** turn right and then left towards Over House. Follow the road to the left and continue until the road turns sharp right, where you go over a stile **B**, GPS 53° 53.821 02° 03.573, and into fields. Cross a stream, go through a gate and climb past Woodhead Farm. Take a right to go around the farm and cross on to the metalled track at the cattle grid. Then take a right to go downhill into Lothersdale **1**, with its wonderfully incongruous tower.

Turn right at the road, over a bridge and into the village. After the Hare and Hounds pub, turn left through a farmyard and up a track, keeping to the left by a hedge. After crossing a road, head north-west along a concrete track and when it turns left (to Hewitts Farm), cross the wall and head uphill, along a walled track, then over a field (where a lamb followed me, heartbreakingly bleating for milk, while its mother watched with a frown).

Across a stile, the route heads left, west, on a slabbed path on to the moor **C**, GPS 53° 55.259 02° 05.178.

Lothersdale: Historical. Pretty. Friendly. Has a pub. What's not to love?

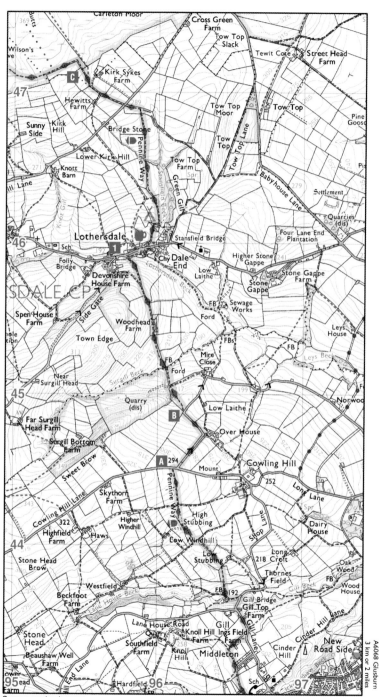

Contours are given in metres
The vertical interval is 5m

You approach the summit of Pinhaw Beacon **2**, today's highest point, with views opening up all around, including the Dales to the north. Soak them up, because they're the last real panoramic views of the day. Here the Pennine chain enters the middle third: from moorland to limestone country.

Two paths lead downhill. Take the right-hand route (they join up anyway) on a clear path past an old quarry and down a track in the direction of the mast. When you reach the road (Colne–Carleton), go straight over and follow a smaller road (Clogger Lane) downhill, north-west.

Where a wall bears left away from the road **D**, GPS 53° 55.434 02° 06.070, the Way passes over a stile. Head downhill following the wall on the right (for Earby, head south-west from here), though a fetching little stretch of moorland may make you want to slow your pace and

Barnoldswick
3 km or 2 miles

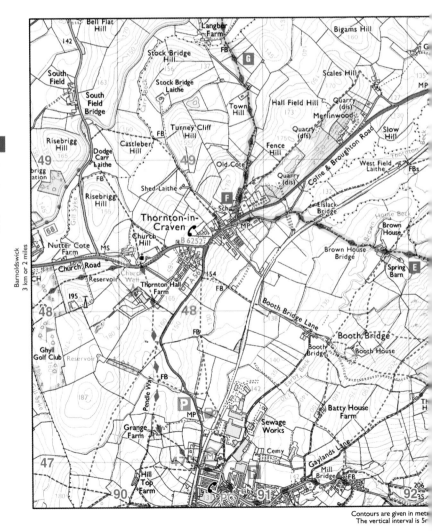

Contours are given in metr
The vertical interval is 5r

linger, especially with the thought of all the flat walking ahead.

After a wall-stile descend until you bear right over a footbridge. Head downhill, with a farm away to your right, towards the verdant valley of Thornton. Cross a stile beside a gate. The path's vague here, but continue down the field past oak trees, keeping to the left to find a kissing-gate at the bottom **E**.

Go through gate and field and follow signs through Brown House Farm (not to be confused with nearby barn conversion Spring Barn) and on to a metalled track. Continue along the track and into the

valley, under a bridge beneath an old railway and uphill into punctilious Thornton-in-Craven.

The Way switches north, across the A56 and up Cam Lane **F**, past some pretty cottages and colourful gardens and to the right of a terrace of old cottages, then along a track to the left of Old Cote Farm. You can see green fields spreading away to the left and, in the distance, Pen-y-ghent throwing down a gauntlet.

Just after a barn, bear half-right, diagonally across a field to the far corner **G**, GPS 53° 56.492 02° 08.435. Go downhill and up again, over the brow of

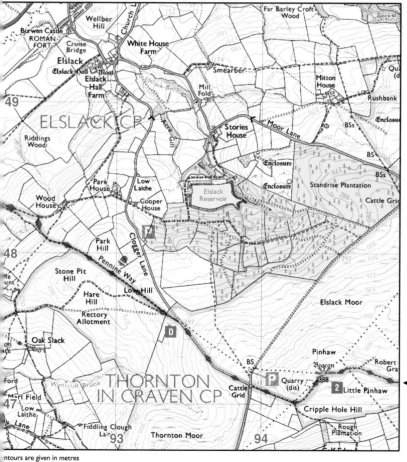

ntours are given in metres
the vertical interval is 5m

Langber Hill, then descend to a stile beside a group of ash trees. Climbing again, go through a gate and right, along the towpath of the **Leeds and Liverpool Canal** 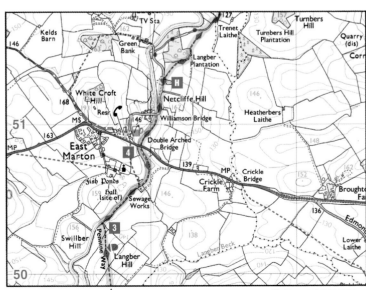.

Follow the towpath, in the shade of beech and sycamore trees, and go beneath a little bridge by a barn. The canal is wider here, as it's an unofficial turning point for 70-foot narrowboats. Swans nest each year in the reeds in front of East Marton Church, on the left.

Around the next canal bend is another bridge **4**, a curious double-decker number, which supports the A59. The upper arch was built on its predecessor to raise the height to the same level as the road.

After the A59, the Way sticks to the towpath until it meets another bridge, where it bears right, up a bank to meet a road. Keep to this little road, ignoring a track to the right, then turn right **H**, GPS 53° 57.463 02° 08.236, through a stile and go diagonally across a pasture through a small gate and briefly into a beechwood.

Carry on (north) across the field and past a crab-apple tree to turn right on to a narrow lane. The canal is only a stone's throw away, but invisible on the other side of a grassy embankment to your left.

Go over a bridge and turn right at a stone stile **I**, GPS 53° 57.693 02° 07.888, and head half-left, uphill on pastureland. Go over the brow with Turnbers Hill on the right, then down to Crickle Beck. From here follow the way across several fields and past Newton Grange Farm. After crossing the beck at a gate **J** head uphill towards a gate and straight on through obvious gates and stiles. Look for a Pennine Way signpost on the brow of Scaleber Hill, with its summit to your left.

The spot basked in sunlight as I approached, but as I went over the crest the dramatic shapes of the Dales loomed up in front of me, cloaked in a far more ominous weather system. It felt like swapping the Shire for Mordor in J. R. R. Tolkein's *Lord of the Rings* and was my favourite moment of the day.

Descend into the wide valley of the Aire Gap, joining a concrete track to cross a railway bridge. About 45 yards (40 metres) past the bridge turn right **K**, GPS 53°

Contours are given in metres
The vertical intervals are 5 and 10 m

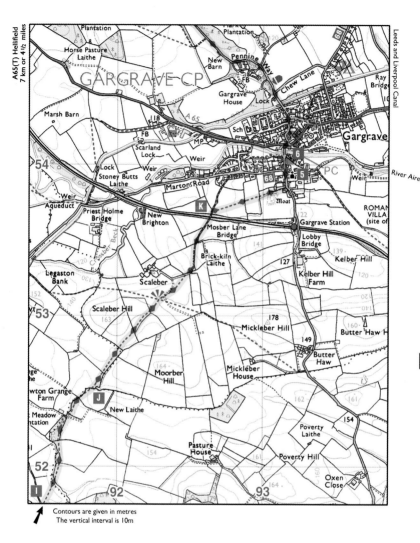

Contours are given in metres
The vertical interval is 10m

58.754 02° 06.821, through a gate and head across fields and through a squeeze-stile in a wall on the outskirts of Gargrave.

Turn right, through a gate, and left along a road in the middle of town. St Andrew's Church **5**, to your right, was reputedly spared by marauding Scots during border troubles because it was named after their patron saint.

Cross the bridge over the River Aire **6** and the main road, then the route heads

north up a side-road, the first turning on the left, just after the famous Dalesman Café, which only the impatient will be able to resist.

Pass the village hall and a car park and bear left up West Street, which continues northwards, over our old friend the Leeds and Liverpool Canal. When the road turns right you again follow a narrower road, which continues north-west around Gargrave House and beside a wood.

The Leeds and Liverpool Canal is the longest canal in Britain built as a single waterway.

Just beyond the wood, bear right over a stile in a wall , GPS 53° 59.453 02° 06.984, then diagonally left over a small brow and down towards another stile , GPS 53° 59.603 02° 07.113, and continue uphill to a post on the edge of an enclosure at Harrows Hill. From here continue north-west across rolling pastureland, down to a stile, then up a broad hill crest to meet a wall, which marks the boundary of the Yorkshire Dales National Park.

Follow the wall all the way to its far-left corner and a signpost , GPS 54° 00.164 02° 07.696, a gate and a stile lead you right, north-west, again towards the not-actually-very-moor-like Eshton

Moor. Take the clear path downhill, along a pretty stretch, to cross several stiles to a wall beside a road . Follow the wall to your left, go through the gate and cross a footbridge across the River Aire.

From here, the final stretch into Malham will delight some and dismay others in its flatness. In summer, beech and willow trees droop protectively over the river and the fields are alive with cowslips and primroses. You may see and hear grey wagtails, dippers, common sandpipers, redshank, curlews and lapwings.

At the Newfield Bridge , GPS 54° 01.132 02° 08.601, the Way crosses to the east bank, passing a weir and

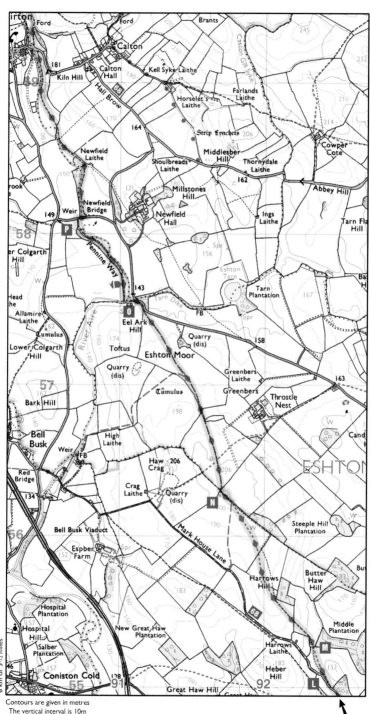

Contours are given in metres
The vertical interval is 10m

That's the spirit. Malham knows how to welcome tired, hungry and thirsty walkers (besides, anyone without muddy boots is clearly cheating).

Leave the river bank at Hanlith bridge , GPS 54° 02.778 02° 09.268, and turn right up the road past Badger House , with its impressive badger weather vane, then climb steeply uphill until the road turns left then sharp right at some farm buildings. Turn off the road here , GPS 54° 02.923 02° 09.093, and left through a small gate into a field.

Over the brow of a hill you can see the dramatic Great Scar Limestone and probably pick out Malham Cove and **Gordale Scar**. Across the valley to the left, old terraces, or lynchets, are still visible, reminders that this has been farming country for thousands of years.

A cairn and a signpost lead you round to the right of a wall above a hanger of mixed deciduous trees. You have clear views of **Malham** now and the route leads downhill alongside a riverside path and into one of the Way's best villages.

It may be of interest to know that Tom Stephenson was born near here – the dashing Dales and limestone splendour were clearly formative.

heading north to Airton . The route continues north, playing an old-fashioned flirting game with the river, which lets itself be chased but veers off again teasingly whenever the two get close. The route is clear to the road at Hanlith.

Transport
Lothersdale (on route)
Earby (1.5 miles/2.4 km)
Thornton-in-Craven (on route)
West Marton (1 mile/1.6 km)
Gargrave (on route)
Airton (on route)
Malham (on route)

Refreshments, public toilets and information
Lothersdale (on route) Hare and Hounds
Earby (1.5 miles/2.4 km) Red Lion
East Marton (on route) Cross Keys, Abbots Harbour Café
Gargrave (on route) Masons Arms, Old Swan Inn, Dalesman Café,
White Cottage Tea Room
Malham (on route) Buck Inn, Lister Arms, Old Barn Café, Beck Hall, Cove Centre
Food shops: Earby, Gargrave, Malham
Public toilets: Gargrave, Malham
Information: Malham (National Park Centre, 01729 833200)

Accommodation
Lothersdale (on route) Lynmouth
Earby (1 mile/1.6 km) Earby YHA
East Marton (on route) Sawley House
Gargrave (on route) Eshton Road Caravan Site
Airton (on route) Airton Quaker Hostel
Malham (on route) wide selection, including camping at Gordale Scar

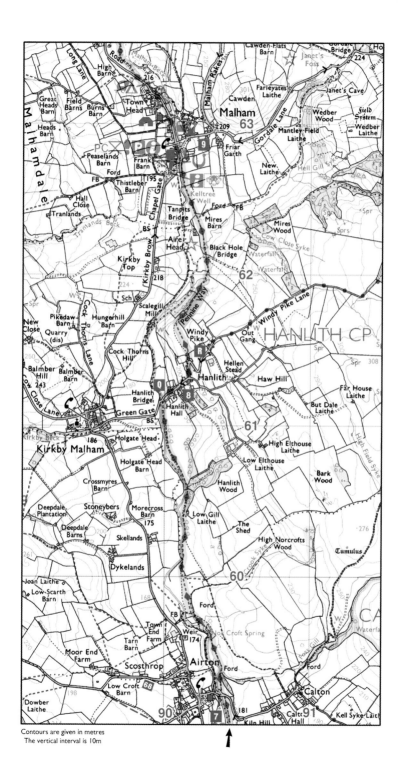

Contours are given in metres
The vertical interval is 10m

6 Malham to Horton in Ribblesdale

around Malham Tarn, over Fountains Fell and Pen-y-ghent
14.5 miles (23 km)

Ascent 2,660 feet (811 metres)

Descent 2,560 feet (780 metres)

Highest point Pen-y-ghent: 2,277 feet (694 metres)

Lowest point Horton in Ribblesdale: 721 feet (220 metres)

This is a special day. Wainwright thought the limestone country around Malham 'the best walkers' territory so far encountered along the Pennine Way' and few would disagree. You're treated to majestic Malham Cove, Malham Tarn and plenty of limestone splendour, before the daunting but curious-looking lump of Pen-y-ghent, the highest point on the Way so far.

It's a challenging day, with two stiff sustained climbs, in the deceptively tough Fountains Fell and not-as-tough-as-it-looks Pen-y-ghent. The latter is certainly worth it for the views, the former is fondly remembered by few. Wainwright described the descent to Horton in Ribblesdale as 'very, very good', but some will find it mildly torturous and interminable.

Route-finding is straightforward, though you wouldn't want to be caught out on Pen-y-ghent in rough weather. Likewise, you wouldn't want to get lost on Fountains Fell, as there are sinkholes and mineshafts lurking, but the path's good.

Be warned that the Yorkshire Three Peaks crowds can make Horton a surprisingly noisy night stop at weekends and there aren't any facilities en route today.

Things to look out for

2 Malham Cove Harry Potter fans may recognise Malham Cove from *The Deathly Hallows* Part 1, where Harry and Hermione set up camp on the limestone pavement of the Cove's roof. The natural amphitheatre has been a limestone luminary for a long time, though. It used to be a huge waterfall and is still a 260-foot (80-metre) sheer cliff. 'The greatest natural feature seen on the whole Pennine Way,' proclaimed Wainwright (before you accuse him of being two-faced, Gordale Scar isn't strictly on the Way). The Cove feels like the wall of an intimidating yet striking castle and it's a popular climbing spot. It may seem logical, but the water that emerges at the cliff's bottom is not from Malham Tarn. A dye was put in the water to test the theory, proving there's no connecting waterway. To one side of the Cove are Iron Age earthworks, low ridges that are ancient field boundaries. To the other side are cultivation terraces, or lynchets, dating back to the Dark Ages. It's a good place to see house martins, too, and even peregrine falcons.

3 **Limestone pavement** When the great ice sheets retreated from around these parts they left flat shelves of white Great Scar Limestone. Carbon-dioxide-carrying rain entered grooves and clefts, cavities were hollowed out and a mosaic of ridges and furrows was formed. There was no soil, so rain disappeared into the ground, feeding subterranean rivers and creating convoluted cave systems, while the surface remained as dry as bone. 'Streams play hide and seek,' wrote Pennine Way mastermind Tom Stephenson. The system of ridges and clefts is known locally as 'clints' and 'grikes', and the technical word for this sort of limestone country is 'karst' or glacial karst. The Yorkshire Dales show this scenery at its very best and there are wonderful examples of pavements above Malham Cove and Gordale Scar. Clint flora includes globeflower, giant bellflower, bloody cranesbill and herb paris, while the grikes are often home to lily of the valley, angular Solomon's seal, dark-red helleborine, mountain avens, green spleenwort and holly fern.

5 **Malham Tarn** A large, beautiful natural lake, Malham Tarn improbably thrives in porous limestone country – a bed of shale helps it out. Wainwright called it an 'enchanted wonderland' and it dates back 12,000 years, to the last Ice Age. Signs proclaim the vast tarn a wetland of international importance and it inspired the Victorian historian and novelist Charles Kingsley's *The Water-Babies* (Lowthwaite in the book is inspired by Malham Cove). Charles Darwin also visited. The woodlands and tarn are a National Nature Reserve, run by the National Trust. This is the only place along the Way that you're able to see the sun setting into the water. Though if you do witness such a thing, you need to get a move on.

19 **Pen-y-ghent** 'Every walker will have his (seemingly Wainwright didn't think walkers would be female) own special favourite memory [of the Pennine Way]. Mine is the sight of the limestone pinnacle of Penyghent [*sic* – he refused to use hyphens, branding them irritating], seen in April sunshine, draped with purple saxifrage.' He argued that it's a mountain not a hill. 'It's rough, stony and almost precipitous on its south and west ridges and it sticks up from the moors like a huge stranded whale on a beach . . . it's an insult to describe it as a hill.' That said, Pen-y-ghent means 'Hill of the Winds', but it is the highest, most rugged test so far on the Way and offers wonderful views. It is part of the Yorkshire Three Peaks challenge (with Ingleborough and Whernside), so it can get busy.

13 **Horton in Ribblesdale** Charming little Horton, with its river, good pubs, a great café and karst scenery, is the perfect reward for a hard day's hiking. The Pen-y-ghent Café is a Pennine Way institution and walkers are invited to sign the book, which goes back several volumes and 40-plus years. The café's also great for re-supplying (including outdoor equipment), information and a good breakfast. The Yorkshire Three Peaks challenge can turn Horton a bit mental, so it's another one to avoid at busy times if at all possible (and book accommodation for a Friday or Saturday). The church has a 16th-century tower as well as some Norman markings.

Don't make the same mistake one guidebook writer made, of thinking either of the two pubs in Horton might have satellite TV. I went hell-for-leather down from Pen-y-gent, getting to the bar with sore feet but in time for my football team's kick-off. . . Only to find neither pub was showing it, instead relying on texts from supporters of the opposition team, who equalised in the 102nd minute. Sore feet and a sore sporting heart.

Route description

From Monk's Bridge **A**, close to the post office and the Buck Inn, the Way heads north along Cove Road, signposted 'Malham Tarn 3'. The route passes the village hall and some pretty cottages to the left, on to a clump of buildings at Town Head **1**, including the 17th-century calamine storehouse, used when mineral was mined in the area. Turn right **B**, GPS 54° 03.879 02° 09.351, off the road, and along a gravel track, towards Malham Cove.

Follow the route along the ash-lined beck towards the rock face, then it turns sharp left to head up over the western shoulder of **Malham Cove 2**. But most will want to head on for a closer look at the Cove's towering limestone cliff.

Afterwards, follow the steep, stepped path up the side of the Cove to a kissing-gate **C** and turn right to cross shelves of **limestone pavement 3**. Don't worry if you lose the precise route here; just head directly for the wall at the other side and a signpost. There are terrific views from up

here, back across your last two days of walking. Even if it seems a little early for a cheeky sit-down, it's very tempting.

There's still plenty of handsome stuff about as you turn left by the signpost and follow the drystone wall and a well-used path up Watlowes Valley **4**. At the top cross a stile **D** and go sharp right, then skirt Comb Hill. Continue over flat limestone grassland, by sinkholes and a stream, which appears and disappears depending on the time of year. Eventually you reach a road.

Turn right, then left at a car park, and stick to the left-hand path to skirt Tarn Foot, leading to a gate and into the nature reserve of **Malham Tarn 5**. The Way follows the track around the tarn towards the wood above the north shore.

You pass Monk's Road **6**, to the right, just before entering the wood. The ancient route was used in the Middle Ages by the holy chaps from Fountains Abbey, who tended sheep and farmed fish around here. Go along the clear track

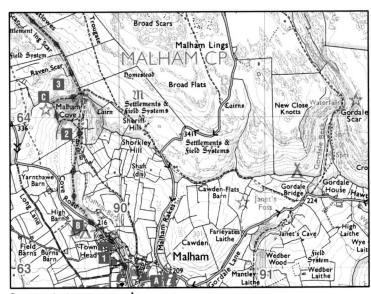

Contours are given in metres
The vertical interval is 10m

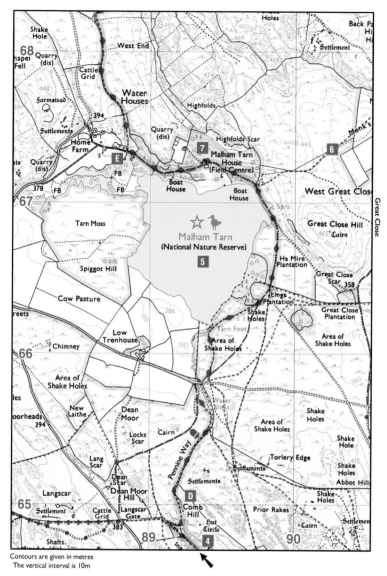

Contours are given in metres
The vertical interval is 10m

through the wood to the big house **7**, managed by the Field Studies Council. Follow the Way through the grounds and continue along the broad track, well shaded, with, amongst other plants, dog's mercury (small green flowers) and enchanter's nightshade (whitish flowers; not to be confused with true nightshade, which can be fatal).

Just before a house on the right, turn right **E** through a gate off the track and on to a grassy path. Go past a line of sycamore, a cluster of limestone boulders and follow drystone walls across several fields, before heading left downhill across pastureland to a road. A ridge of redoubtable fells rises in front of you, including Fountains Fell.

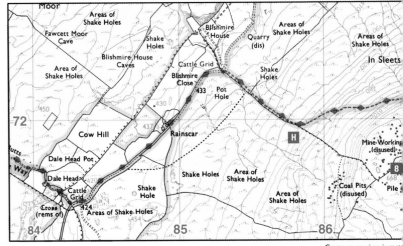

Contours are given in metr

Go across the road and through a kissing-gate 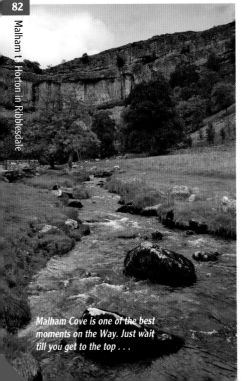 F, GPS 54° 07.081 02° 10.703, beside a cattle grid, then along a track to Tennant Gill Farm. Pass to the left of the buildings and head straight up the hill behind, climbing to a step-stile. You've just swapped the beguiling green pastures of limestone country for your old friend/fiend the bleak moors, and an arduous, frustrating climb up Fountains Fell lies ahead.

Bear left, then turn right to reach an old wall line and climb uphill. After keeping straight for a while, angle right G, GPS 54° 07.527 02° 11.426, and climb on a mine track (there are potentially hazardous ex-mines and so forth around, so try not to stray far from the path), then on a newly built path.

There are several false summits to taunt you as you climb, finally, to two huge cairns. (The real summit lies to the south-west 8 amid a field of cairns and long-abandoned colliery pits.) From here you can see the Yorkshire Three Peaks: Ingleborough, Whernside and your next opponent, Pen-y-ghent.

Indeed Pen-y-ghent dominates your view as you cross a stone stile over a wall. It's an easier climb than it looks from here, though. Descend down a rocky path, which eventually meets a wall H and turns right, north-west, and straight down to a road.

Turn left on the road, cross a cattle grid and head south-west, past Rainscar. Walls around here are built from stones first

Malham Cove is one of the best moments on the Way. Just wait till you get to the top . . .

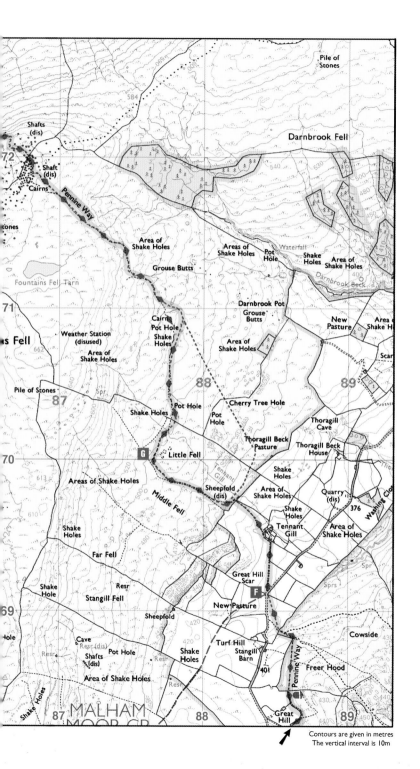

Contours are given in metres
The vertical interval is 10m

gathered by prehistoric settlers. After another cattle grid turn right. Just after a deep crater to your left – called Churn Milk Hole **9**, a classic honeycombed cave – it's right again, GPS 54° 08.542 02° 15.206, along a track. The path gains height gradually and crosses a stile. You're now head to head with your enemy, **Pen-y-ghent 10**. The route is obvious and the steep section actually fairly short, even if one guidebook writer needed a moment or two to stop and, ahem, 'admire the view'.

Before you know it you're on the summit plateau and it's a gradual ascent to the summit trig point, at 2,277 feet (694 metres). Wonderful views make the sweaty armpits worthwhile.

From the trig, go over the wall to the left and descend down a clear path that soon swings right, north. Turn sharp left at a junction **I**, GPS 54° 09.811 02° 15.042, to begin a steeper descent on a surfaced

path. Eventually the path levels and you bear right to meet a gate and stile.

A web of paths spreads in all directions **J**, GPS 54° 09.845 02° 16.360, including a track heading north to the epic underground cavity Hull Pot **11**, the largest natural hole in England and a famous pot-holing spot. But the Way goes through a gate, left down an obvious green road between two drystone walls. A little way along, on the left, is Tarn Bar **12**, a mini version of Malham Cove, and beneath it a pretty valley.

The track loses height with frustrating slowness and does an excellent impression of a treadmill. Bear right at a fork **K**, GPS 54° 08.880 02° 17.466, which brings you to the B6479 (Selside) road. Turn right (unless you're hot-footing it to the Golden Lion, in which case turn left) to the bright lights of **Horton in Ribblesdale 13**.

Wainwright argued Pen-y-ghent, one of the Yorkshire Three Peaks, is a mountain not a hill.

Public transport

Horton in Ribblesdale (on route) ⇌ 🚌
Settle (6 miles/9.6 km) ⇌ 🚌 🚍

Refreshments, public toilets and information

Horton in Ribblesdale (on route) 🍺
Golden Lion Hotel, Crown Hotel; ☕
Pen-y-ghent Café, Blindbeck Tea Room

Food shops: Horton in Ribblesdale, Settle
Public toilets: Horton in Ribblesdale, Settle
Information: Horton in Ribblesdale
(Pen-y-ghent Café, 01729 86033)

Accommodation

Horton in Ribblesdale (on route)
wide selection
Settle (5 miles/8 km) wide selection

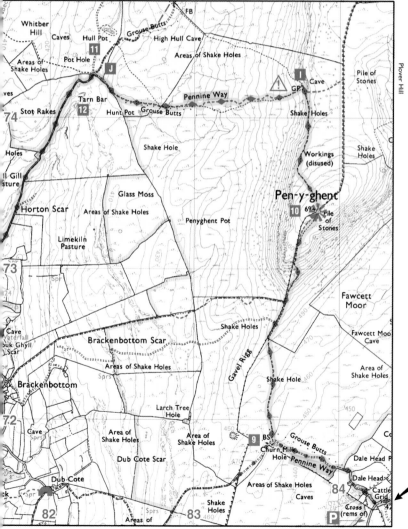

Contours are given in metres
The vertical interval is 10m

7 Horton in Ribblesdale to Hawes

over Cam Fell and Dodd Fell
14 miles (23 km)

Ascent 1,760 feet (536 metres)
Descent 1,727 feet (526 metres)
Highest point Tan End Cam Fell: 1,870 feet (570 metres)
Lowest point Hawes: 1,092 feet (333 metres)

Though there may not be any obvious highlights today, this is a very enjoyable section of the Way. It's not too testing physically, route-finding is mostly easy and the views are plain wonderful. Though you follow old packhorse routes and Roman roads, you'll see few signs of contemporary civilisation, instead mainly endless hills with grass swishing in the wind as a long, gentle ascent takes you over the Dales to a more abrupt drop into charming Hawes, the pot of gold at the day's end.

Some may find it lonely and exposed, but the big skies, empty trails and wide-angle views are blissful, especially after the bustle of Malham and Horton in Ribblesdale. It was one of my favourite days and even Wainwright used the word 'exhilarating' in his description.

Navigationally, most of the day could be sleepwalked. But there's an awkward part coming off the moors down Rottenstone Hill into Hawes, where the path is a bit vague. There are no facilities till Hawes, which has everything you could wish for and more. Though if you'd rather stay somewhere quieter, perhaps push on to Hardraw.

Things to look out for

Packhorse routes Much of today's walk follows old packhorse routes over the Dales. These were once thriving horse-ways (though strictly speaking it was usually ponies) carrying wool, coal, iron and more down from the moors to the towns. The routes were often chosen to evade local taxes and toll roads and they became well-trodden paths. When alternative forms of transport became more popular, the routes became the domain of farmers. They too switched to more advanced modes of transport, meaning walkers now rule the paths.

Karst scenery A glacier once flowed south towards Horton in Ribblesdale, widening the cleft in the land – the valley you'll see down to your left in the morning – and exposing shoulders of limestone. When the ice retreated it left drumlins and erratics (ridges and boulders) and the weather set to work on the naked rock. The other side of the valley is home to some of the most impressive bits of limestone pavement in the Dales. The word *karst*, incidentally, derives from Slovenia.

3 Ling Gill Nature Reserve This pretty little oasis in a deep limestone gorge may have been part of ancient sub-alpine forest mostly wiped out by farming. It's dominated by ash trees, but also has rowan, aspen, birch and hazel. Rare flora, such as alpine cinquefoil, grows on the slopes, not forgetting the wonderfully named melancholy thistle. Even without going into the reserve itself, it's possible to spy St John's wort, thyme, lady's bedstraw and wood cranesbill.

Ribblehead Viaduct The charismatic piece of architecture is a symbol of the railway age, but also of spirited social action. The 24-arch viaduct is part of the Settle–Carlisle line. It's 0.25 mile (0.4 km) long, 104 feet (31 metres) high and was completed in 1875, having taken five years to build. In 1981 the line was under threat of closure, partly because it was thought the old viaduct was beyond repair. Friends of the Settle–Carlisle Line (FofSCL) was formed and the 3,000-strong protest group stuck it to The Man. In 1989 the line was finally saved, the viaduct repaired and the route re-opened as a historic and scenic train journey. If you get a chance, it's a lovely trip. FofSCL still has 3,500 members today.

Wensleydale cheese Hawes is also home to Wensleydale Creamery, which makes the cheese of Wallace and Gromit fame. In fact, the tasty foodstuff, which dates back to the Cistercian monks in 1150, was struggling until the films made the cheese an international hit. Tours are available, but the famous cheese isn't made every day so call ahead. I carefully carried some Wensleydale cheese home all the way to the south Cotswolds, only to find it's sold in my local shop.

10 Hawes This is a place you make a mental note to come back to when you're accompanied by a more civilised aroma. Welcoming cafés, outdoor shops (stock up on waterproofer), three pubs, an irresistible market (Tuesdays), ATMs, a chemist and a wood-shelved health-food shop make it feel like a relative metropolis – certainly one of the best-equipped places on the Way. All that, with the gorgeous backdrop of those buxom Dales and, somehow, without ruining its small village charm. By now at least one walker coming in the opposite direction should have tipped you off about the chip shop, which has the best fish and chips on the route. The Dales Countryside Museum is also excellent and the Ropemakers is well worth a peek.

The Ribblehead Viaduct is an arresting sight, but also a triumph against The Man.

Route description

In Horton in Ribblesdale, head north along the B6479, past the café and over a bridge towards the Crown Inn, where you turn right **A** into the car park. Bear left up a pretty, walled green road lined with clover, lady's mantle and water avens. You'll see views of barns and meadows, classic Dales scenery, with the titans of Pen-y-ghent and Ingleborough above the shelves of Great Scar Limestone on either side of the dale.

You gain height gradually, passing Sell Gill Holes **1** to your right – a vast underground cavern and another big draw for pot-holers. Go through a gate and enjoy views of limestone scars and terracettes,

plus some clints and grikes (ridges and clefts) **2** over the wall to the left. Jackdaw Hole, another cave, is nearby.

Follow the track along the green road, usually beside a drystone wall, with shake holes and other grassy cavities to the right. Eventually the Way crosses a stream and goes through a gate **B**.

Continue along the track and through another gate. Then turn left **C**, away from the track, up over the brow of a hill, with the conifer plantation to the right. Head down to a low saddle, with the wonderfully named Dismal Hill (sounds as if Wainwright named it) to the left, then bear left on a track past the farm at Old

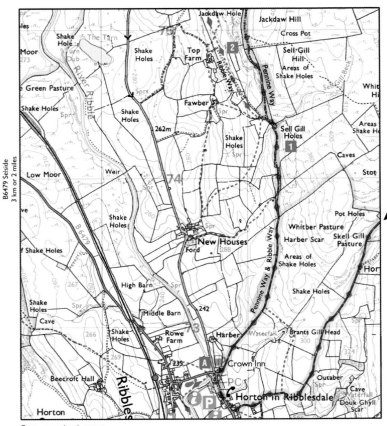

Contours are given in metres
The vertical interval is 10m

Ing. Bear right before a gate, following a walled track on an old **packhorse road** to another gate and stile.

Keeping north, the Way contours round Cave Hill and Fair Bottom Hill to meet Ling Gill ③. Through the gate the path descends to cross Ling Gill Bridge ④,

GPS 54° 12.348 02° 18.209, whose barely legible inscription reads 'ANNO 1765 THYS BRIDGE WAS REPEAIRED AT THE CHARGE OF THE WHOLE OF WEST DYDEING'. After crossing it, follow a track uphill, then wind north, rising all the time across open moorland.

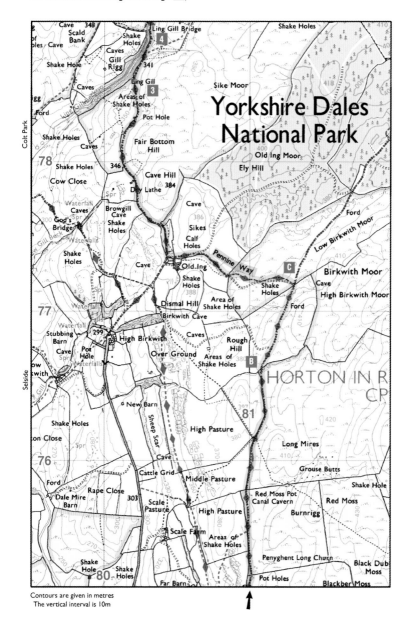

Contours are given in metres
The vertical interval is 10m

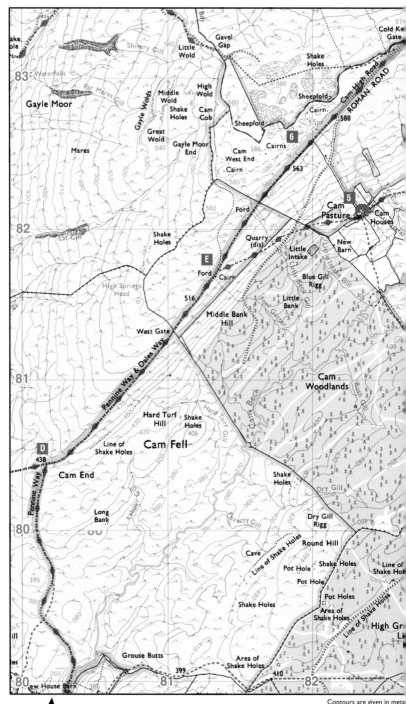

Horton in Ribblesdale to Hawes

Contours are given in metr
The vertical interval is 10

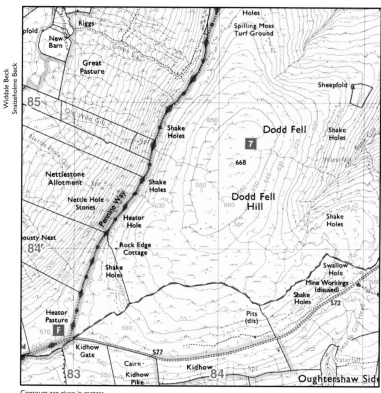

Contours are given in metres
The vertical interval is 10m

Like yesterday's approach to Fountains Fell, the bridge marks a change from limestone to moorland. You may have already spied the **Ribblehead Viaduct** away to your left and soon you'll have even better views of it, along with Three Peak Country.

Eventually the path meets a junction with the Dales Way **D**, GPS 54° 13.164 02° 18.336. The two trails team up for a while to form a well-worn thoroughfare over Cam Fell. Once called the Cam High Road by wool traders, this route was also used by Romans and, very likely, by those who came before them. Cam House **5** is the only settlement visible, but the path is easy to follow. Before Cam House, however, the Way bears left at a fork **E**, GPS 54° 14.414 02° 16.514, marked by a cairn, up on to the Roman road.

Continue to climb for a while, then the route levels off, with a beautiful valley to the right and a limestone edge **6** to the left. When you meet a metalled road, follow it then bear left **F**, GPS 54° 14.757 02° 15.767, on a track by a Pennine Way signpost. This is the old packhorse route called West Cam Road and travelling along it, in this barren but untamed and beautiful landscape, made me forget my aches and pains and release a big smile. There was nowhere I'd rather be.

The concealed Snaizeholme Valley opens up to the left, with homely woods, dancing streams and an atmosphere of unselfconscious beauty. It seems the perfect place to retire to, or maybe hide out from the law (not an immediate concern, but you never know). To the right an aloof Dodd Fell **7** towers to 2,192 feet (668 metres).

The journey into Hawes, and the best fish and chips on the Pennine Way.

As you head north-east along the ancient track, you're leaving limestone country behind. Just before the main track goes round a corner, take a signposted right turn, GPS 54° 16.637 02° 14.555, uphill to Ten End **8**. You're soon following the remains of an old wall. Around the corner rewarding new vistas open up to the east, across to Sleddale and Wether Fell. Ahead is the inviting valley of Wensleydale – the only one of the principal Yorkshire Dales not named after its river – and beyond that Great

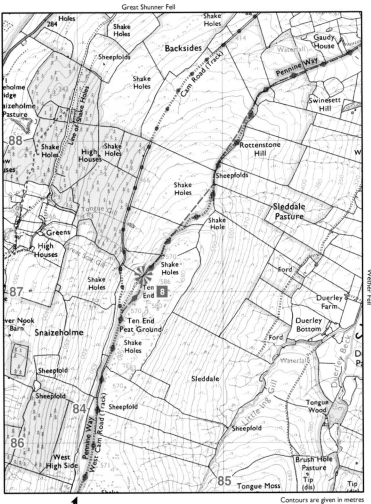

Contours are given in metres
The vertical interval is 10m

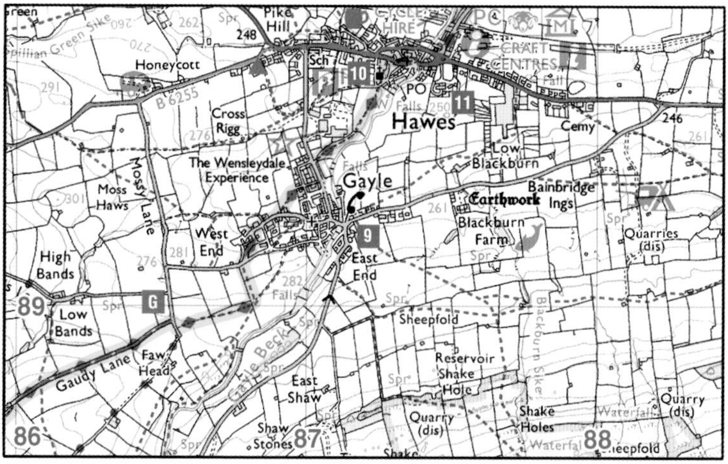

Contours are given in metres
The vertical interval is 10m

Shunner Fell, your next opponent, with Buttertubs Pass and well-named Lovely Seat to its right. Happy days.

The Way becomes a grassy path that descends sharply down Rottenstone Hill. Pay attention here or you'll soon be off route (though in unfriendly weather, simply continuing downhill should see you right eventually). The path goes through remnants of a wall heading north-east. Coming over a small stony ridge, head down to cross a stream and meet a wall. Go through a gate and continue down, using the wall as your guide. After a gate, follow another ruined wall to big cairns and another gate. Follow the tumbling-down wall, then, after a gate, a better wall (to your left) before joining a walled track (Gaudy Lane) just after Gaudy House on the left. Continue to a road and turn right **G**, GPS 54° 17.758 02° 12.503, then immediately left, and through two hayfields, turning left downhill to the west end of the village of Gayle, which has Celtic origins.

On the road take the first left and go down a lane opposite, through an estate. This is the modern end of Gayle – its old bridge **9** can be seen on a short detour. Turn left into a small field, then follow the narrow walled path through the housing estate. The Way turns left along a road, then right and along a pretty path of stone slabs above the Gayle Beck, with the old mill and bridge visible to the south. Follow the path to the right of the St Margaret church **10** and on to the main street of **Hawes** **11**.

You've now completed 100 miles (160 km) of the Pennine Way. But most of the best bits are still ahead of you . . .

Public transport

Hawes (on route)
Garsdale Station (6 miles/9.6 km)

Refreshments, public toilets and information

Hawes (on route)

Food shops: Hawes
Public toilets: Hawes
Information: Hawes (National Park Centre, 01969 666210, hawes@yorkshiredales.org.uk)

Accommodation

Hawes (on route) wide selection

8 Hawes to Tan Hill

over Great Shunner Fell and along Swaledale
16.5 miles (27 km)

Ascent 3,005 feet (916 metres)

Descent 2,346 feet (715 metres)

Highest point Great Shunner Fell: 2,349 feet (716 metres)

Lowest point Thwaite: 984 feet (300 metres)

There's no two ways about it: today is a Pennine Way classic, stating a convincing case for getting into that prestigious shortlist of Pennine Way Top Five Days.

After the finest waterfall on the Way, a gradual but thrilling climb takes you on to the moors and over Great Shunner Fell, the highest point on the walk so far. (In a rare moment of good humour, Wainwright said he could climb Great Shunner 'nonstop' despite being 'senile and getting as fat as a pig'.) Up here, more than ever before, it can feel like you're walking the backbone of England. The Way leads down to cute little Thwaite and along the dashing cleft of Swaledale and to Keld, via some waterfalls, where the Way crosses its rival, the Coast to Coast Walk (remember to boo and hiss at the walkers doing that one). A steep but short ascent takes you back on to the moor, to end with a night to remember in one of the Way's most legendary pubs. Ladies and gentlemen, we've hit the motherlode.

Attention needs to be paid between Thwaite and Swaledale to avoid a wrong turn; the last leg on the moors could be troublesome in bad weather and Great Shunner is an exposed place in rough weather.

Sustenance stops are tempting in Thwaite and Keld (only a few minutes off route), where the day could be shortened.

Things to look out for

2 Hardraw Force The massive centrepiece of little Hardraw is this fairytale waterfall. At over 98 feet (30 metres), the vertical wall of wet stuff, plunging from the head of a limestone gorge, is the highest single-drop waterfall above ground in the country. It's well worth the short detour through the Green Dragon Inn – a lovely pub, parts of which date from the 14th century – and the £2 they'll charge you. You can walk behind the waterfall, though be very careful on wet rocks. Now is not the time for your best impression of Daniel Day-Lewis in *The Last of the Mohicans*. Talking of the big screen, the waterfall featured in *Robin Hood: Prince of Thieves*. Famous 19th-century tightrope-walker Charles Blondin crossed the ravine on a wire here, apparently stopping halfway to cook an omelette. Perhaps don't try this either.

4 Thwaite This is arguably the prettiest settlement along the entire Way. The name, like the old village, is of Norse origin and means a clearing in the trees – 'fell', 'scar' and 'gill' are Norse names too. The Kearton Country Hotel and Tea Shop is named after the Kearton brothers, Richard and Cherry, sons of a gamekeeper, who spent their formative years in Thwaite. Born in the 1870s, both became famous as naturalists, but Cherry Kearton was also a pioneer wildlife photographer and conservationist. Richard, who was disabled, was a lecturer and the two collaborated on many wildlife books.

■ **Meadows and barns** You're about to see a lot of photogenic little hay barns. Modern farming methods have killed off many native wild flowers in Britain. Silage-making means cutting the grass early in the season, removing flowers before they've set seed, while fertilisers are harmful too. Farmers around here used to wait until high summer to cut the hay, which allowed the flowers a full cycle of growth. There aren't many authentic meadows left in Britain now, but the Yorkshire Dales is one of the few places where whole landscapes of flower-rich meadows survive, along with their lonely barns, which used to house a few head of cattle per field. Meadow flowers show their happy colours for a very short time each year and in early summer you might see meadow buttercup, bulbous buttercup, globeflower, eyebright, meadow saxifrage, wood cranesbill, dovesfoot cranesbill, ragged robin, common sorrel, red clover and northern marsh orchid.

7 Swaledale and Keld As you climb up on to the moors after Keld, the view back shows how ice has shaped the land. Kisdon Hill was probably an island. The site of Keld was submerged beneath meltwater, which then split to head south-east along the main Swaledale and south along the course of what is now the tiny

Skeb Skeugh, to meet again at Muker. The cobweb of fields on the lower slopes and the ancient names for the settlements suggest early farmers were quick to recognise the area's potential, although Swaledale was always isolated. 'Keld' means 'a place by a river' in Norse and it is most people's idea of a classic Dales village: small, picturesque and hospitable. Keld is a last glimpse of dreamy Dales scenery, before the Way climbs to rugged moorland and County Durham.

9 Tan Hill Inn Once the meeting place for four packhorse trails, this inn dates from the 17th century. Now it's more famous for being Britain's highest pub (1,732 feet/528 metres above sea level), for its unusual dispute with Kentucky Fried Chicken and for starring in TV commercials for double-glazing. In 2007 the inn was asked by KFC to remove the words 'family feast' from its Christmas menu. Owner Tracy Daly thought the letter was a late April Fool's joke. It was genuine, but the inn stood its ground and subsequently KFC confirmed it would not be pursuing the case. No pub this remote should be this popular, and that probably has much to do with the boisterous and highly entertaining landlady. A night here is a great chance to catch up with fellow hikers trading tips and blisters.

When Wainwright got here, 'soaked and squirting water' as he researched his guidebook, it was closed. 'This was the only occasion in a long career of walking that I sought refuge under an umbrella,' he said, 'and a lady's at that. Afterwards I did the honourable thing and married her.'

I sat eating dinner here, thinking I was the only hiker in the pub. But as conversations wore on and overlapped between tables, it turned out there was no one here but hikers, including a few strays from the Coast to Coast. Probably my best evening on the Way.

Route description

In Hawes turn left down the road just before the Dales Museum (opposite the pedestrian island with the statues). Cross a bridge **A**, then turn left and quickly right through a backpack-mashing kissing-gate into a field on flagstones. Back on the road (with sweet cicely along the verges), cross the River Ure by Haylands Bridge **B**.

Take the second left **C**, off the road and along a footpath signed Pennine Way, and you're soon following a causey-flagged route through meadows to Hardraw. You meet the road again at a bridge **1** across a beck and from here you can pop to the Green Dragon, opposite, to see **Hardraw Force 2**.

Across the bridge, in the shade of cherry trees and horse chestnuts, past a tea room, turn right **D** off the road at a slate-sided house. The footpath is signposted and begins on a walled drove road, although you are soon on the open fell, where the atmosphere begins to change. Buttercups give way to tormentil and swathes of mat-grass (*Nardus stricta*). Keep looking back to see some wonderful views open up, with Ingleborough on the skyline.

The stony track is quite steep – ignore other paths to right and left. Clumps of thyme grow on limestone shelves, in summer attracting the mountain bumblebee and the heath butterfly.

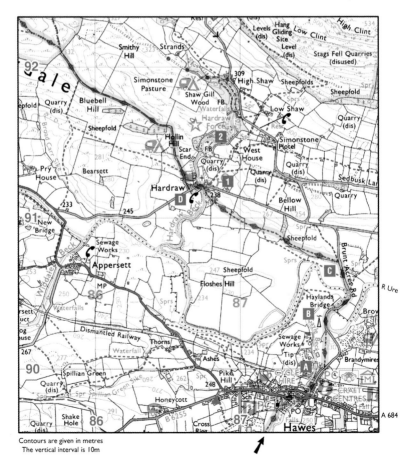

Contours are given in metres
The vertical interval is 10m

On the shoulder of the fell at Hearne Top there's a fork 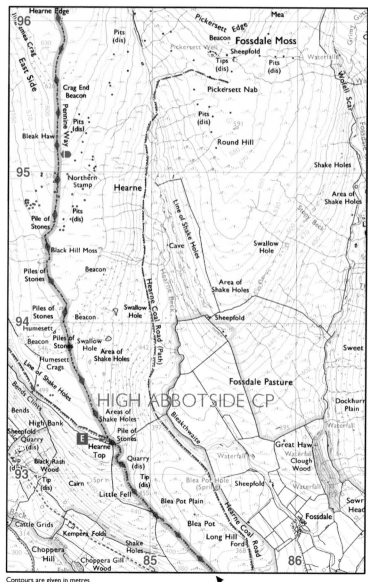, GPS 54° 20.071 02° 14.221, and the Way arcs right to keep with the main ridge. Again, ignore side paths; if in doubt just stick to the ridge and look for occasional cairns. Apart from sheep, the only signs of life are skylarks, pipits, wheatears, golden plovers and curlews. Further up, you may spy rare dunlin in summer. They like high ground, especially boggy moorland.

Continue onwards and upwards on a long climb past Crag End Beacon (a neat pile of stones) to another shoulder at Hearne Edge.

Contours are given in metres
The vertical interval is 10m

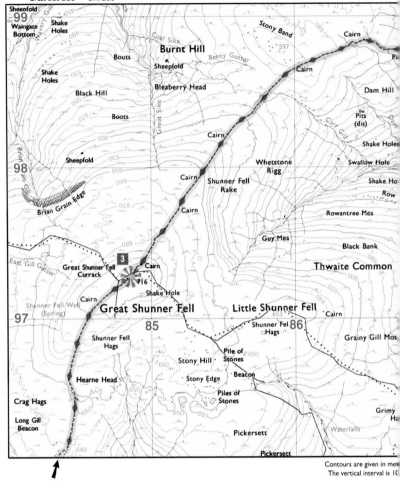

Contours are given in met

The vertical interval is 1C

This is a glorious stretch and it can feel as if you're walking along the backs of humpback whales, like something out of a Roald Dahl story. This is the Way at its best: remote, beautiful and exposed – meaning if it was windy down in Hawes it'll be blowing a hurricane up here: tie everything down!

The summit of Great Shunner Fell **3** (2,350 feet/716 metres) has a four-way stone wind-shelter and commands wonderful, almost endless views in good weather, including to the Lake District's 'magic mountains' (as the partisan

Wainwright put it) to the west and even to Cross Fell, the Way's highest point, still two days' walk away.

From the summit the route crosses a fence and heads north-east, dropping gradually to Beacon Cairn, GPS 54° 22.614 02° 13.620, then more sharply over marshy ground, which is often stone-slabbed. Sleddale and Birkdale ('birk' is the old name for birch) can be seen to the left, while to the right is the valley of Thwaite Beck, leading into Swaledale.

The path arcs right, eastwards, on stone slabs and eventually meets the top of a

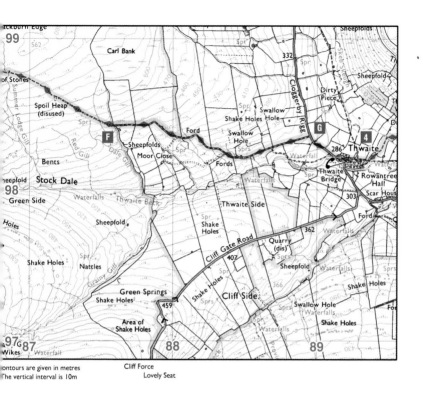

Contours are given in metres
The vertical interval is 10m

Cliff Force
Lovely Seat

walled drove road **F** with fields on both sides. Look back as you descend to see Great and Little Shunner standing side by side like unaccommodating nightclub bouncers – quick, hurry on before they notice you've snuck past.

The route downhill towards Thwaite follows a steep, stony track, which in midsummer has beautiful flower-filled meadows on either side. When the track meets a road turn right **G**, past some field barns, and follow the road down into **Thwaite 4**.

Entering the village, take the first road on the left, past the Kearton Country Hotel and Tea Shop, which offers an opportunity for a pot of tea not to be dismissed lightly.

You'll find arguably the Way's cutest village well worth the Thwaite.

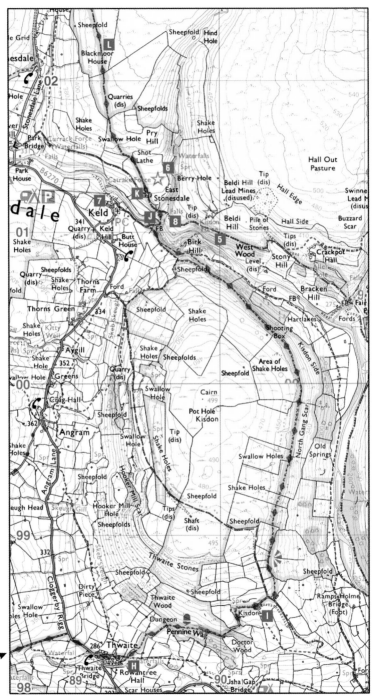

Contours are given in metres
The vertical interval is 10m

Carry on to a stile beside a cottage, then follow a walled path and more stiles to bear left over meadowland, with Kisdon Hill rising steeply in the background. Wainwright thought the next segment the most beautiful so far. 'If only the whole of the Pennine Way were as pleasant as this!' he said. After crossing the lower meadows, turn left after a stile and begin to climb steeply, as the path becomes stony with patches of bilberry, cow wheat and thyme. The view back is excellent: the village surrounded by a network of wobbly lined walls with Great Shunner rising protectively behind.

The view ahead will soon be pretty special too, but pay attention here and look for signposts, as the next section can be confusing. The Way takes a rather convoluted route around fields to a house, where you should ignore the track and inviting valley in front of you (this is not the valley you're looking for) and go left uphill on a walled track around another field. Head north along the shoulder of Kisdon Hill, above the steep slope of North Gang Scar, then north-west, following the contour of the valley.

At Birk Hill the route drops below a cliff face where there are clumps of hart's-tongue fern, whitlow grass, pearlwort and shining cranesbill. Kisdon Force lies immediately below and the opposite hillside carries the East Gill Beck and its little waterfall.

The path is stony and sometimes over scree, so tread carefully. But route-finding is straightforward now, usually following the tumbledown wall, through woodland and downhill, to a meeting with the Coast to Coast Walk. Both routes cross the river and the village of Keld , a potential overnight stop, lies a few hundred yards to the north.

The route passes East Gill Force , a pretty little waterfall and one of four along a geological fault-line. The other three are off route, but worth a nose if

you've time. Downstream, Kisdon Force is arguably the most spectacular – Wainwright called it 'a place for lovers' – while Catrake Force and Wain Wath Force make themselves heard upstream.

Bear left on a steep track up to East Stonesdale Farm. Past the farmhouse the Way continues uphill along a grassy track (not on the tarmac track, which marks the Coast to Coast route westwards). As you go uphill look back to soak in the views. 'Leave this charming scene with regret,' wrote Wainwright. 'Nothing as pleasing will be seen for many a long mile.' And for once, he's not wrong.

The brief encounter with the other long-distance trail triggered some nostalgia for me, having walked it a few years previously. Though, because of its glorious moors, lack of crowds and some spectacular treats in store further north, I can safely say I prefer this one.

Go along a walled drove road, but once past a gate and barn you settle down to a long and gradual ascent through rough out-pasture. Head north on a shoulder of West Stonesdale, with Birk Dale away to the left.

Looking back to see Kisdon Hill, near Keld, which was probably once an island. Cherish such views because the scenery's about to change . . .

Again you'll find the Way can switch from green and pretty surroundings to bleak and hostile habitat with alarming ease. Soon the only signs of human endeavour will be the side road across the valley – which you could walk along if conditions are hostile and/or you're worried about getting lost – and the grassed-over remains of lead mines and coal pits (so be careful).

After a short walled section and a last barn by Mould Gill, the route angles more steeply uphill and you begin to bear right and cross a bridge 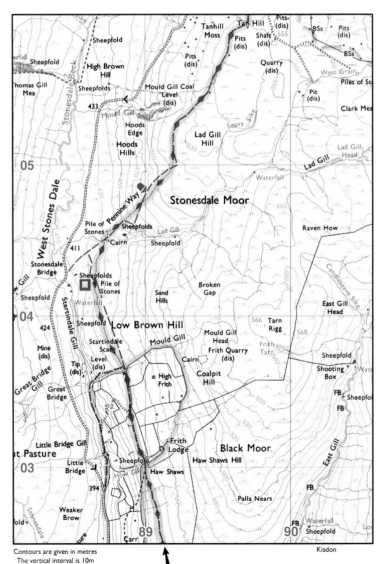, GPS 54° 25.999 02° 10.581, to go uphill, north-east, following a groove in the hillside of Stonesdale Moor.

The track is cairned and you follow an old packhorse trail across a wild, remote stretch of moorland. Go left on a stony track, as the

Contours are given in metres
The vertical interval is 10m

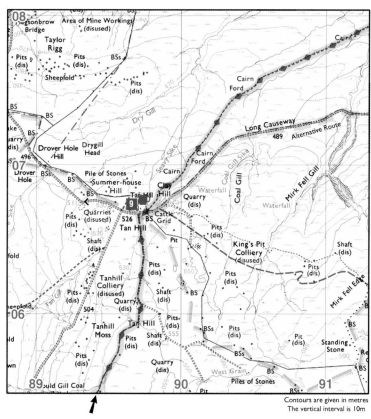

Contours are given in metres
The vertical interval is 10m

isolated **Tan Hill Inn** 9, quite possibly the loneliest-looking pub you'll ever see (the moor around the Pack Horse Inn looked a tad more friendly), lies ahead. It's hard to imagine a more welcome sight.

This area is pockmarked with colliery workings, mainly from the 19th century but some of them nearly 600 years old, so perhaps avoid the idea of any midnight strolls after a few ales.

Public transport

Thwaite (on route) 🚌🚐
Muker (1.5 miles/2.4 km) 🚌
Keld (0.3 mile/0.5 km) 🚌

Refreshments, public toilets and information

Hardraw (on route) 🛏 Green Dragon Inn; 🍵 Cart Horse Tea Rooms
Thwaite (on route) 🍵 Kearton Country Hotel
Muker (1.5 miles/2.4 km) wide selection

Keld (0.3 mile/0.5 km) 🍵; 🛏 Keld Lodge
Tan Hill Inn 🛏
Food shops: Muker, Keld

Accommodation

Hardraw (on route) Green Dragon Inn, Shaw Ghyll Campsite, Simonstone Hall Hotel
Thwaite (on route) Kearton Country Hotel
Muker (1.5 miles/2.4 km) wide selection
Keld (0.3 mile/0.5 km) Park Lodge, Keld Bunkhouse & Park House Campsite, Keld Lodge, Butt House
Tan Hill Inn (on route)

9 Tan Hill to Middleton-in-Teesdale

via the Stainmore Gap
17 miles (27 km)

Ascent 1,614 feet (492 metres)

Descent 2,280 feet (695 metres)

Highest point Tan Hill: 1,732 feet (528 metres)

Lowest point Middleton-in-Teesdale: 892 feet (272 metres)

Is it heartening or disheartening to know that today finally marks the halfway point of the Pennine Way? Likewise, this is the sort of day that divides opinion. Some will begrudge the trudging over endless, often squelchy, moorland, most likely with soggy feet. Others will relish the heather, the views and the mood changes of the unceasing stretches of peat and purple heather.

There are several picturesque pieces of countryside along the way, including verdant valleys, a Bronze Age burial site – traders from that era used the Stainmore Gap as they did the Aire Gap, Romans too – and a castle (sort of). A lot of wall following, a great navigation aid, can feel like a rehearsal for the stretch on Hadrian's Wall. But on the downside, fellow members of the anti-reservoir brigade (an increasingly vocal lobbying group) will be gritting teeth today.

Similar to coming down into Hawes, the route of the day's final leg around and down Harter Fell isn't always clear, but in most weathers it would be hard to get properly lost. Though the harder ascent, over Lundedale, has been meanly saved for the latter end of the day.

There aren't any lunching options, but the day could be made shorter by stopping at Baldersdale, or detouring to Bowes before that. In fact, the Bowes Loop, an official variant from Trough Heads Farm, exists for those wanting to stop off there, or to cut the Way in half and return (with dry feet) to finish it off another time.

Things to look out for

1 Sleightholme Moor Even fans of the bleakest, most barren moorland will find it difficult to warm to Sleightholme Moor. 'On my death bed I may well murmur the words "Sleightholme Moor" involuntarily as I expire,' said Barry Pilton in *One Man and His Bog*. It's boggy, treacherous, the path isn't always obvious and if your boots dried out properly overnight you're about to find out what a waste of effort that was.

Wainwright said the moor was 'like walking in porridge', or, after heavy rain, oxtail soup, and he labelled this stretch 'a journey of despair'. I wouldn't disagree and I soon had wet feet. However, my morning was brightened up by one of the Tan Hill Inn dogs following me for several miles. A phone call was needed to arrange a collection point and a lift back for the runaway grouse-bothering scamp.

3 Bowes Moor Wainwright called this 'the greatest wilderness in the country'. He added: 'This is a no-man's-land, a region that never appears in the headlines nor even in the small print.' The moor shows its best colours in August and September when the heather is in glorious flower. May and June, meanwhile, are brought to life by golden plovers and curlews, and some impressive insects, including emperor, fox and northern eggar moths.

4 Hannah's Meadow Hannah Hauxwell was a solitary Daleswoman who found unlikely celebrity in the 1970s through a TV documentary about her life on an isolated farm where she lived without electricity or running water. She went on to ride the Orient Express and meet the Pope. Because her pocket of land was managed without the use of pesticides, herbicides or fertilisers, it contains several plants, such as wood cranesbill, globeflower, ragged robbin and adder's tongue fern, which have disappeared from other meadows in the area. It is now a Site of Special Scientific Interest, owned by Durham Wildlife Trust, and a converted barn provides more information about Hannah and the Trust.

8 Kirkcarrion As you start to head down into Middleton-in-Teesdale, you're likely to spy a knoll at the end of the ridge to the right (east). This is Kirkcarrion, a Bronze Age tumulus or burial site, now planted with pines. For centuries people have avoided it and locals talk of seeing ghosts here.

9 Middleton-in-Teesdale Coming down into the Teesdale valley is one of the prettiest and most inviting ends to a Way day. Charming and friendly Middleton-in-Teesdale is a Saxon settlement which expanded dramatically in the 18th century when the Quaker Company – the London Lead Company – opened mines in the area. The tiny town has a full range of facilities, with some good-looking B&Bs, pubs, cafés and restaurants, plus banks, food shops, etc. The church has a 16th-century detached campanile or belltower,

an architectural rarity. An out-of-character Wainwright said the town promised 'beds and breakfasts, pretty girls, fish and chips, beer, ice-cream. Yipee!' By the sounds of it he was already sampling the local sauce.

12 Bowes The Romans built a fort here to defend the road linking Watling Street at Penrith with Dere Street (which you'll meet again in the Cheviots) at Scotch Corner. The site of the fort, named Lavatrae, was used again in the 12th century by the Normans and was subsequently squabbled over by kings (including Henry II), terrorists, archbishops and outlaws. By the mid-14th century, predictably, it was a ruin – but a ruin that still stands today, known as Bowes Castle. Bowes' significance doesn't end there. At the end of the main street an unusual square house used to be a school and in 1838 a visitor called Charles Dickens, England's most quintessentially Victorian author, was so affected by the harsh regime at the institution that he caricatured it as Dotheboys Hall in *Nicholas Nickleby*. William Shaw, the original Wackford Squeers, and George Ashton Taylor, who is thought to have inspired the character Smike, are buried in the churchyard close by. Visitors may find the Bowes Museum and historic Bowes Railway worth a visit, too.

Hannah Hauxwell: an unlikely celebrity in the 1970s. Organic farming pioneer, stubborn traditionalist, or both?

Route description

Turn left out of the Tan Hill Inn on to the road, then left again at the cattle grid **A**. You've just left Yorkshire and the Yorkshire Dales National Park and are now in County Durham, of which your first taste is unlikely to be favourable: welcome to **Sleightholme Moor 1**.

In bad weather this can be a dangerous place and you could use an alternative route: follow the road for 2 miles (3 km) before turning north-east at Great Cocker **B** to follow Sleightholme Moor Road (a track) to meet the Way beyond Hound Beck.

On the official path, the going is difficult on this wasteland of untrustworthy, spongy,

boggy peat and the route sometimes unclear. Look for white-tipped wooden posts at first, which sadly become less regular, but continue on in the same direction, keeping the Frumming Beck on your right. Look for a sheepfold **C** (small stone structure), GPS 54° 27.968 02° 08.250, and directly ahead in the far distance is Sleightholme Farm.

The Way crosses a series of wooden bridges and a big stone cairn, GPS 54° 28.085 02° 07.920, before crossing a green bridge **D** to join a track, which meets another track **E**, GPS 54° 28.738 02° 05.528, leading to Sleightholme Farm.

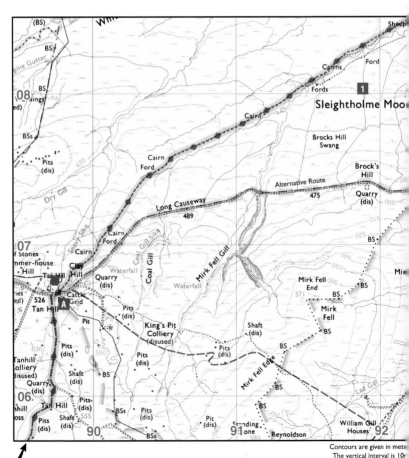

Contours are given in metr
The vertical interval is 10r

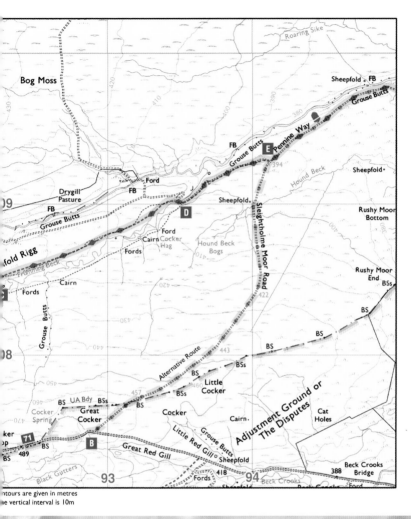

Roaring Sike

Bog Moss

Sheepfold · FB
Grouse Butts

Pennine Way

FB
Grouse Butts · **E**

Sheepfold ·

394

Hound Beck

Drygill
Pasture   · Ford

FB

Sheepfold ·

Rushy Moor
Bottom

FB
Grouse Butts

D

Sheepfold.

Ford
Cairn Cocker
Hag

Hound Beck
Bogs

Sleightholme Moor Road

Rushy Moor
End   BSs

Fords

fold Rigg

Frumming Beck

Cairn

Fords

Grouse Butts

422

BS

BS

Adjustment Ground or
The Disputes

Alternative Route   443

BS

BSs

BS

Little
Cocker

BSs

Cocker

Cairn.

Cat
Holes

BS UA Bdy BSs

457

460

BS

Cocker
Spring

Great
Cocker

Grouse Butts

Little Red Gill

ker   **71**

489   BS

BS   **B**

Great Red Gill

Sheepfold

Beck Crooks
388   Bridge

Black Gutters

93

Fords   418

94   Beck Crooks

Sheepfold   Beck Crooks · Ford

...ntours are given in metres
...he vertical interval is 10m

107

Tan Hill to Middleton-in-Teesdale

...he bright lights of Sleightholme Farm – an oasis of sophistication and culture amongst all that sogginess.

After the farm and past Kingdom Lodge, the Way turns left through a gate and across open pasture down towards a mini version of Malham Cove and Intake Bridge 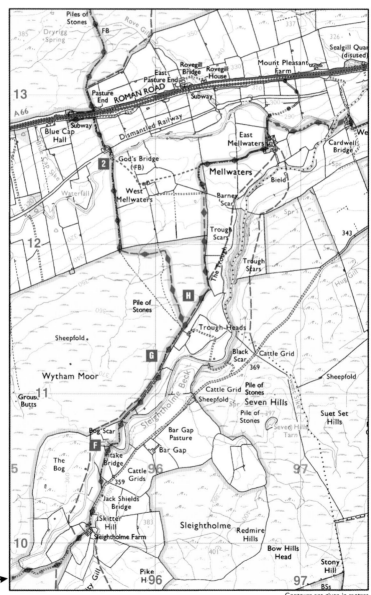. Across the water a path leads steeply uphill, with a pretty little valley to the right, to follow a route parallel with Sleightholme Beck towards Trough Heads Farm. Bear left through a gate , GPS 54° 29.740 02° 03.764, on to the moor and continue beside the wall to , GPS 54°29.890 02° 03.627, a signpost where

Contours are given in metres
The vertical interval is 10m

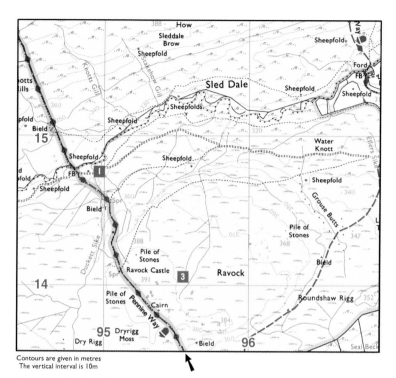

Contours are given in metres
The vertical interval is 10m

the route splits. If you're continuing to Middleton-in-Teesdale, turn left and head north. If you're going to Bowes, the route continues north-east; see pages 114–15.

From the signpost where the route splits, turn left and head north, then follow a wall left (north, then west) across heather moorland to a bridle-gate. Go through the gate and follow the wall downhill, after which the Way is obvious down to the River Greta at God's Bridge 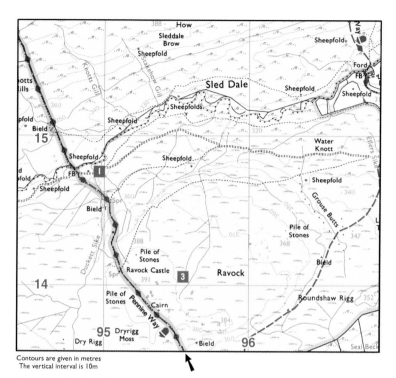. This natural phenomenon, where the river disappears beneath a great slab of limestone, has been used for many centuries.

On the north side of the Greta you climb a punishingly steep track towards the A66, where an underpass takes you safely beneath the busy trunk road. The A66, through the Stainmore Gap, is a route that dates back to the early Bronze Age (1600 BC at least) and is probably the most historical road crossed by the Way. Romans, Vikings and Normans all used it too.

Head towards the house named Pasture End, then go uphill to the left of it, following the wall. The route up on to **Bowes Moor** is a little vague, but watch for cairns as it bears north-east towards the bracken-covered slope of Ravock, before turning back north-west to make for a cairn and the ruins of a stone hut called Ravock Castle. The site is underwhelming if you were expecting a castle and, perhaps a little harshly, a seemingly piqued Wainwright called it 'a pathetic ruin'. (If you're really annoyed, there's a better castle in Bowes.)

Once over the crest of the hill, aim for the large brown hut (which has a walkers' shelter/lunch hut at one end). Then, after a concrete footbridge over the dark waters of Deepdale Beck, a straight wall on the far side of Deep Dale marks the route back uphill.

Once across Deep Dale, go through a gate and follow a path beside a drystone wall,

Tan Hill to Middleton-in-Teesdale

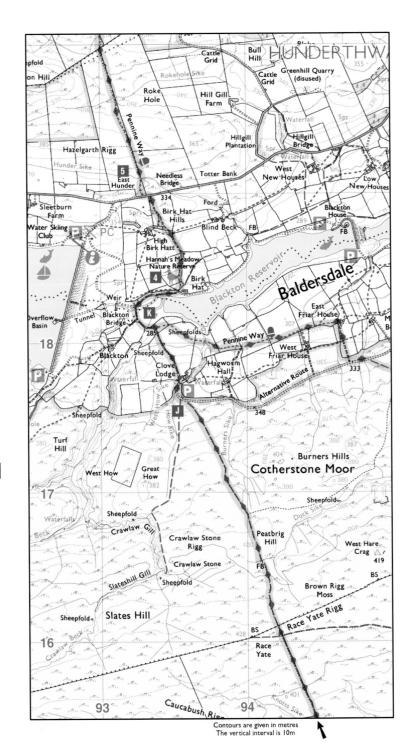

Tan Hill to Middleton-in-Teesdale

Contours are given in metres
The vertical interval is 10m

Coming down from Cotherstone Moor, on a day without A-list highlights. Some may find it boring, others blissful . . .

climbing via a testing trudge and several false crests to Race Yate Rigg. On this broad ridge the wall is left behind and Bowes Moor merges into Cotherstone Moor.

In rain or mist, this sweep of featureless badlands could be daunting and you might want to reach for the compass, but in good visibility Baldersdale and its reservoirs (grr) are in sight. The route descends along a straight path across grassy, mossy moorland, keeping well left of the curious mounds of Burners Hills to meet a road just south of Clove Lodge Farm **J**, GPS 54° 33.226 02° 06.035.

The Way continues north along the road and down to Clove Lodge. Go through the gate, across the yard and bear left, then downhill to cross a little bridge with a stream and the reservoir to the right.

This is where the Bowes Loop rejoins the official Pennine Way route. More importantly, perhaps, Baldersdale marks the halfway point of the Way.

Head north over the larger Blackton Bridge **K**, with the grassed dam wall of Baldershead Reservoir and a nature reserve to the left. The Way goes through Birk Hat, where a road leads left then uphill through pastures and meadows, including **Hannah's Meadow** **4** on your left.

At a road, turn left then right to get off it and uphill again over rushy pasture. On the brow of the hill **5**, GPS 54° 34.146 02° 06.396, there are views ahead over Lunedale, Teesdale and Hunderthwaite Moor to the left. The route drops down into the Lunedale, following a wall at first, then leaving it to cross a stile at a gate in the bottom wall, aiming for the farm buildings of Beck Head.

There is a path diagonally across meadows towards the road at the brilliantly named How. Two reservoirs lie below. Some of Grassholme's marshy shallows are a nature reserve **6** and in spring and summer a large colony of noisy blackheaded gulls take up residence here.

At the road the Way bears right, then quickly left around a farmstead. Walk down to cross the reservoir at a bridge **L**,

then climb the road to Grassholme Farm **M**, turn right through it and north along a clear path. The Way leads up through meadows and eventually to a road. Go directly across it to a track leading to Wythes Hill Farm. Follow the walled track (ignoring a sign and gate on left) across a stream and through a gate, and diagonally

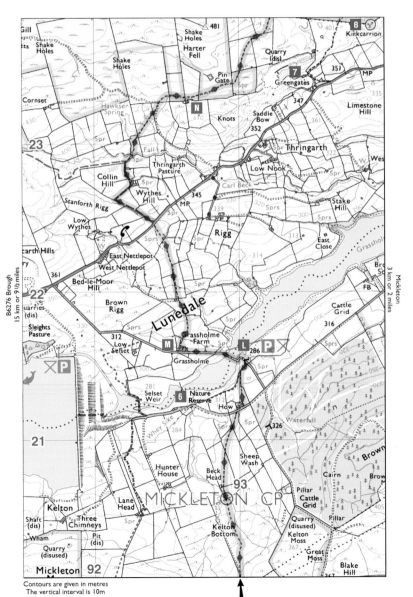

Contours are given in metres
The vertical interval is 10m

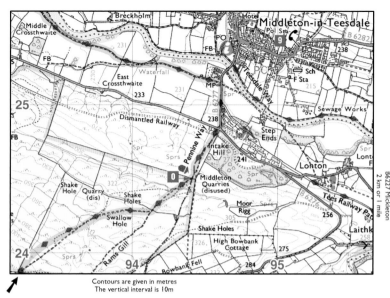

Contours are given in metres
The vertical interval is 10m

uphill, north-east then east, over rough pasture towards a field barn .

Around here the route is a little vague, but the going is easy as you contour around Harter Fell. To the south and south-west are the high fells of Yorkshire and Cumbria, while in front of you are the meadows and pastures of Teesdale and Lunedale.

Cutting the corner of the ridge, with old quarry workings to the right , the Way stays on the middle contour of the hill through several walled pastures before dropping down on a grassy path, heading north-east towards Middleton-in-Teesdale. The knoll at the end of the ridge to the right, east, is **Kirkcarrion** .

On a sunny evening, this slow, picturesque descent reminds you what the Pennine Way is all about. I felt exhilarated but tired, looking forward to a well-earned feed in a charming village I would probably never have visited otherwise. And dry socks.

The cairned path heads down over pastures to a gate in the field corner , GPS 54° 36.943 02° 05.286, then continues more steeply to cross an old railway embankment and on to a side road. Turn right then left along the B6277

towards Middleton. The Way doesn't enter the village, turning left just before the bridge. But marvellous **Middleton-in-Teesdale** is too tempting not to visit.

Public transport

Bowes (4.5 miles/7 km)
Baldersdale (on route)
Middleton-in-Teesdale (on route)

Refreshments, public toilets and information

Bowes (4.5 miles/7 km) Bowes Museum
Middleton-in-Teesdale (on route)
Rumours Café Shop, Café 1618;
Forresters, Conduit, Teesdale Hotel
Food shops: Bowes, Middleton-in-Teesdale
Public toilets: Middleton-in-Teesdale
Tourist information: Middleton-in-Teesdale (01833 641001)

Accommodation

Bowes (4.5 miles/7 km) Ancient Unicorn, Clint House Farm, West End Farm (camping)
Baldersdale (on route) Clove Lodge
Lunedale Highside Farm (camping)
Middleton-in-Teesdale (on route) wide selection

The Bowes Loop

Heading towards Bowes, the route continues north-east, following a wall (rather than the river) bearing north downhill. Turn right towards East Mellwaters Farm when you meet a track, then left to circle the farm before turning left in the yard past sheds. Continue close to the river and to the left of a wall, crossing Cardwell Bridge and going round West Charity Farm. From here you should be able to see the 12th-century Bowes Castle 10 ahead.

Go through Lady Myres Farm, but before the next farm at West Pasture, turn left off the track, GPS 54° 30.444 02° 01.446, and head down to the river bank. Cross the footbridge near the weir P and climb the path up to Swinholme. A metalled track veers north, but halfway along turn right over a wooden fence, by a signpost, and head east across a field to a gate, then over more fields, to cut across the grass-covered remains of the Roman fort of Lavatrae 11. A slight detour after the gates will take you around the neighbouring ruins of Bowes Castle before continuing along a narrow side road to the main street of Bowes 12.

To get back to the Way from Bowes, a tarmac road crosses the busy A66 and heads north-west uphill over moorland.

Here, military notices appear warning of various dangerous things and Wainwright called this stretch 'the ugliest mile on the Pennine Way'. The Way leaves the road to the left at a stile and bears right, north-west, along a track, through a gate and into open pasture.

After a ruined barn, a path bears west-north-west above Levy Pool 13, then drops down to pass close by the farm, where a track leads through a gate below outbuildings. The Way crosses the bridge over Deepdale Beck and heads north. At Q it crosses grassy ridges towards the Hazelgill Beck; it's marshy and white posts are a good guide. The area to the east of the wall is Ministry of Defence land. Once through the gate R there are lovely views across the moorland.

The Way heads north-west, making to the right of the gritstone outcrop of Goldsborough S. The route is vague again here and a compass is useful. Continue west-north-west, below the face of Goldsborough, then angle northwards over the crest of the ridge to pick up a path north-west and down to Baldersdale and a road.

The official route turns left here, then right along a drive T to East Friar Farm, then west to the end of Blackton Reservoir. Just beyond Hagworm Hall, the obvious path of the direct Pennine Way route leads out on to the road from the left U and you're reunited with your leader.

Day 10 would be in most Wayfarer's Top Three Days on the Way. It starts off from Middleton-in-Teesdale gently, with some joyous riverside walking.

10 Middleton-in-Teesdale to Dufton

past High Force, Cauldron Snout and High Cup
21 miles (34 km)

Ascent 1,837 feet (560 metres)

Descent 2,001 feet (610 metres)

Highest point Rasp Hill: 1,902 feet (580 metres)

Lowest point Dufton: 590 feet (180 metres)

There's no two ways about it: today is Pennine Way gold. The sort of day that lives long in the memory after the walk is done.

Are you in the mood for waterfalls? The suddenly generous Way has three fine specimens for you. And if you're not fussed about falling walls of wet stuff, this leg includes High Cup as its magnificent climax, arguably the best sight along the entire Pennine Way. Actually, there's no arguably about it.

It's an unusually flat day; in fact there's more descent than ascent. For a welcome change, the Way starts with a lovely, leisurely amble through pretty, flower-dotted meadows and beside the chorusing River Tees. 'A walk of near perfection,' said Wainwright. Upper Teesdale ushers you through a picturesque valley before a testing scramble by Cauldron Snout. The stretch before that, too, is a time to watch your step, as it's rocky and sometimes slippy. Then it's over the moors and, the only tricky bit of navigation, to your long-overdue appointment with Nick. It's a long day, but a great one.

If it seems greedy to squeeze so much into one day, you could break it up in Forest-in-Teesdale or Langdon Beck, which are just off route, though to some they'll come too early. Both have (limited) accommodation choices and you could lunch at the Langdon Beck Hotel.

Two more things worth knowing: after sticking fairly doggedly to the east side of the Pennines, today finally deposits you on the western side; in doing so, however, because you've travelled west-south-west you'll be further from Kirk Yetholm than when you started out this morning. But the detour is well worth it.

Things to look out for

■ **Whin Sill** As you follow the River Tees, on your right, in the morning, you'll soon see an escarpment of quartz-dolerite to your left. This ribbon of rock extends across northern England and forms some of the most impressive scenery of the Pennine Way. Whin Sill helps form today's waterfall bonanza, High Cup, parts of Hadrian's Wall are built atop it and you'll even meet it again in the Cheviots.

■ **The Tees and its waterfalls** You're going to get to know the Tees well today. The name probably comes from a Viking legend which talks of a 'boiling, surging river' and the mighty watercourse starts on Cross Fell and flows eastwards for about 85 miles

(137 km) to reach the North Sea between Hartlepool and Redcar. Low Force is the first of the three waterfalls; it's the smallest, the most gentle and graceful too. A little further along, the Tees takes a reckless but joyous leap off a 70-foot (21-metre) dolerite cliff, crashing down into a gorge. 'The greatest waterfall in the country,' said Wainwright. 'No other has so dramatic yet beautiful a setting.' Wainwright thought it the Tees's finest moment and it's hard to disagree. On the other side of the bank you have to pay and join the crowds to get a photo, so you can feel a tiny bit smug about being on the side of the free. High Force isn't England's highest waterfall but it is often reported to be the country's most powerful and also labelled the country's 'biggest' (though the exact criteria remain unclear – isn't Hardraw bigger?). The day's third spectacular water feature is Cauldron Snout, which is fed by the controversial Cow Green Dam and is very different again in character. It's angrier than the other waterfalls (perhaps because of the damage the dam caused?), an explosive gush of water escaping indignantly from a narrow cleft in the Whin Sill, as if powering free from a POW camp. That's after sliding, twisting and squirming for 70 yards (64 metres) down the hillside. For waterfall fans, days don't get any better than this.

■ **Upper Teesdale's wild flowers** Wild flowers from this region are world renowned and that's thanks to a unique habitat. A carpet of tundra vegetation covered most of Britain after the last Ice Age, but was shaded out by trees when the climate improved – except here. Teesdale was most likely a grassy island in a sea of forest and its unique plants have resisted farming and, so far, various climate changes too. The most famous Teesdale plant is the rare spring gentian – a tiny, low-growing and short-lived perennial which produces a five-petalled, vivid blue flower. Another rarity, the Teesdale violet, grows on broken limey ground, especially near molehills, and is smaller and pinker than other violets. Bird's-eye primrose is another beauty; its pink and the pastel shades make it one of the prettiest of plants. Teesdale is a National Nature Reserve, so random trampling is frowned on. It would be a tragedy if a plant had survived for 10,000 years only to be murdered by a clumsy boot.

M **High Cup (Nick)** It's almost as if an earthquake is happening. The ground suddenly opens up beneath you to reveal a terrifying chasm. This apocalyptic cleft, a symmetrical U-shaped valley of sheer whinstone cliffs and dolerite crags, was gouged out by a glacier (or a giant ice-cream scoop) as if to leave a reminder of the awesome power it can wield. Looking down, it's around 700 feet (200 metres) to the valley floor and views to the west go into the Eden Valley and on to the Lake District. Strictly speaking, the stunning landmark is called High Cup; Nick is one particular cleft, on the northern bank. A pinnacle on the right is known as Nichol's Chair, after a local cobbler who climbed the stack and repaired a pair of boots on its summit. Bleedin' show off.

2 **Dufton** This charming settlement in the aptly named Eden Valley is a slice of England you may think had long vanished. A delightful village green, friendly locals, garden gates overhung by roses and honeysuckle, a picturesque backdrop and an air of comfortable prosperity that seems more West Country than Westmorland. Anglo-Saxon in origin, the village Quaker Company – the London Lead Company – had a part to play in its history (like Middleton-in-Teesdale) and Dufton prospered as a lead-mining village. The red sandstone houses are a trademark characteristic, as is the unusual old water pump on the village green.

Contours are given in me
The vertical interval is 1

Route description

Head back out of Middleton on the road you came in on and turn right after some buildings, just after the Tees bridge **A**. To start with the path stays away from the river bank. After a while, when it goes uphill slightly, go to the right of a cairn. Where Rowton Beck meets the Tees **B**, the Way at last drops down to the river and follows it for some time, making navigation simple – a relaxing stroll in pretty meadows. Dippers, grey wagtails, common sandpipers and goosanders can be seen along here, while the alder and sallow bushes are full of willow warblers, blackcaps and redstarts.

Past Scoberry Bridge, you come to Wynch Bridge **1**, England's oldest suspension bridge. It was first erected in 1704 for miners to go from their Holwick homes to the lead mines of Durham, though the current version dates to 1830. Then the path enters Moor House Upper Teesdale National Nature Reserve, GPS 54° 38.635 02' 08.760. The 88 square kilometeres include plenty of rare wild flowers and is a leading site for research into climate change.

You soon see Low Force **2**, a tasty aperitif for what's ahead (be careful taking photos, as people have been known to fall in).

The Wynch Bridge is thought to be Britain's oldest suspension bridge and the current version may date to 1830. But don't worry, you don't have to go over it.

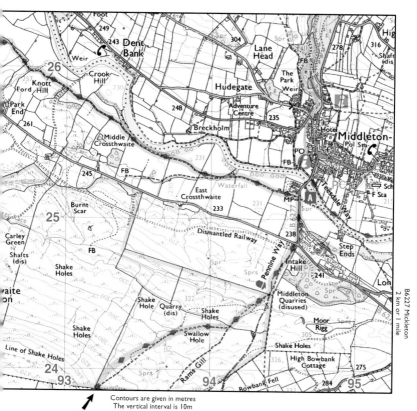

Contours are given in metres
The vertical interval is 10m

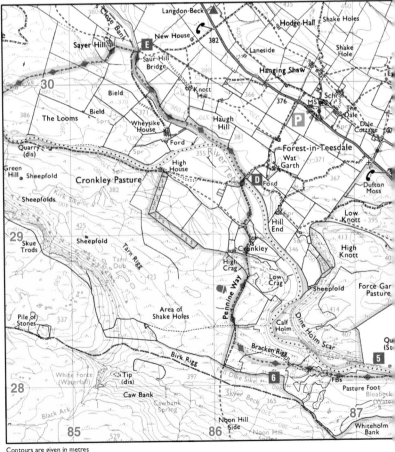

B6277 Alstone
25 km or 15½ miles

Langdon-Beck
Hodge Hall   Shake Holes
Close Bank
New House
Sayer Hill   E
Laneside   Shake Hole
382
Saur-Hill
Bridge   Hanging Shaw
Bield   Knott   376   Sch
Hill   MS   The
30   Dale
Bield   Haugh   Dale Cottage
The Looms   Wheysike   Hill   P
House
Quarry   Ford   Forest-in-Teesdale
(dis)   Wat
Green   High   Garth   Dufton
Hill   Sheepfold   House   D   Ford   Moss
Sheepfolds   Cronkley Pasture   Hill   Low
End   Knott
Skue   Sheepfold   Cronkley   High
29   Trods   High   Low   Knott
Crag   Crag   Sheepfold   Force Gar
Pasture
Pile of   Area of   Calf   Dine Holm Scar   Qu
Stones   Shake Holes   Holm   (St
Bracken Rigg   5
Birk Rigg   6
White Force   Tip   FBs
(Waterfall)   (dis)   Pasture Foot
28   Caw Bank   Bleabeck
Cawbank   Noon Hill   (Wat
Black Ark   Spring   Side   Whiteholm
85   86   Noon Hill   87   Bank

Contours are given in metres
The vertical interval is 10m

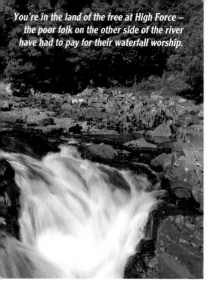

woodland beside the top of High Force (another photo op). The Way continues upstream and the drums die away to be replaced by the call of sandpipers, oystercatchers and redshanks; soon it's hard to imagine what you just saw.

On the opposite bank, a big slice of the hillside has been hacked away by a quarry **5**. Beside this is Dine Holm Scar, decorated by heather and juniper. On the route, Bracken Rigg **6** requires a steep little climb and the Way contours to the left side, via two stiles over fences. Head right and downhill on flags by a stone marker and at the end of the flags turn right through a small gate in the wall.

The Way continues beside a wall, then down a steep, tricky gully to Cronkley Farm and round to its left. From here a track heads north to a bridge **D** and the Way continues on the north bank of the Tees, past the confluence with Harwood Beck.

You could detour to Forest-in-Teesdale here, or to Langdon Beck, about a mile further on at the next bridge, Saur Hill Bridge **E**. From the bridge, the Way

Further on, just past Holwick Head Bridge, the Way climbs along a path to a stile **C**. After Keedholm Scar **3** you begin to hear a distant sound of heavy tribal drumming and soon High Force **4** can be seen by following a short path to the right.

Once you've got your prize-winning photos, the Pennine Way leads out of the

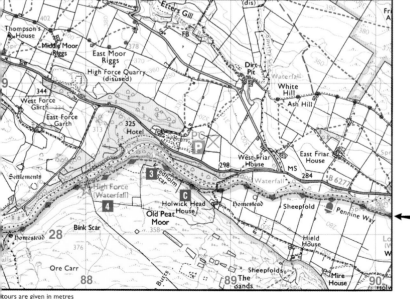

ours are given in metres
vertical interval is 10m

follows a track to Saur Hill Farm ('Sayer Hill' on the map), but angles left and uphill in front of the farm (a relief, as the dogs didn't sound very welcoming) as the Way switches direction, heading south-west. Continue over a wall, then bear right along a vague path across meadowland, over a step-stile, across pastures and past a National Nature Reserve sign, making for the gap to the north (right) of Cronkley Fell. You're soon back with your new friend, the River Tees, which is often accompanied in summer by piping sandpipers and redshank.

The Way stays faithful to the river, passes an inviting bench and carries on to a track 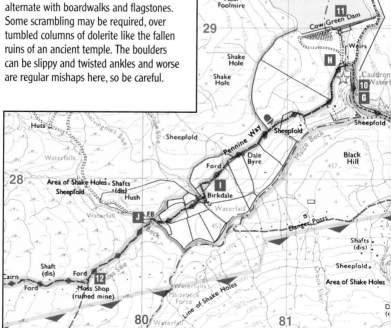 going past the whitewashed Widdy Bank Farm 7. Now a base for Natural England, the farm dates back to 1698 and was part of the Raby estate, thought to stretch most of the way to Darlington. Cronkley Scar, on your left, used to be quarried for lead pencils manufactured in this valley.

A little further on, scree and boulder-fields alternate with boardwalks and flagstones. Some scrambling may be required, over tumbled columns of dolerite like the fallen ruins of an ancient temple. The boulders can be slippy and twisted ankles and worse are regular mishaps here, so be careful.

You'll probably need all eyes on the path, but the rocky slopes and cliffs (or 'clints') to your right 8 are a good place to spy ring ouzels, which are shy, with a distinctive white crescent mark. Round the corner, Falcon Clints 9 are worth a viewing too, and kestrels are often seen around here, as are peregrines and merlins.

The Tees meets Maize Beck G, just before the roar of Cauldron Snout 10 and then the waterfall comes suddenly into sight.

You can enjoy the view of the Tees H from the top, albeit after a testing (especially with a backpack), hands-on scramble. Here you'll also see the large and ugly dam(n) wall of the Cow Green Reservoir 11. Finished in 1970, an area of rare flora was sacrificed for the reservoir and Wainwright called it 'an object of shame and regret'. If you face the other way, the top of Cauldron Snout is still an

Middleton-in-Teesdale to Dufton

Contours are given in metres
The vertical interval is 10m

inviting place to stop for a lunch break. That is, if the midges don't take a fancy to you, which seems arbitrary (they consider guidebook writers a particular delicacy).

Cross the Tees and say goodbye to it as you enter Cumbria on a metalled track, heading west, then south-west towards Birkdale. There are rewarding views back along the upper Tees. Stephenson thought the stretch from here to the Eden Valley 'the wildest and loneliest crossing in the whole of the Pennines'. Though it does have a giant treat in store.

Go through the farmyard at Birkdale **1**, GPS 54° 38.734 02° 18.304, and once

across the bridge at Grain Beck **J** the walk changes as east becomes west.

The path leads to a cairn by a mess of rocks called Moss Shop **12**, GPS 54°38.445 02°18.942, and then swings right. 'Shop' was the name given to very basic bunkhouse accommodation provided for miners on the fells. Cracking views from here include Mickle Fell across Maize Beck to the south-east and Meldon Hill rising in the north-north-west.

From Moss Shop there are flagstones for a bit, then the path becomes vague and following it needs close attention. After a while the trail becomes stony and easier

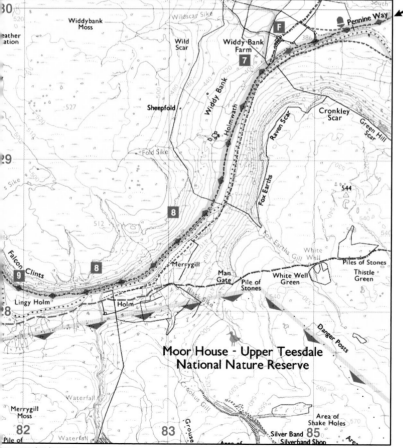

Contours are given in metres
The vertical interval is 10m

The tinkling tranquillity of the river is about to be destroyed by a spitting, snarling beast . . . Cauldron Snout.

to detect, but if in doubt continue in the same direction. There are some posts and cairns as you head up Rasp Hill and signs to your left warn of a military firing range. The most reliable guides are the small clapper bridges over the side-streams. The landscape is bleak and the only sounds likely to be heard are the calls of larks and pipits, curlews and golden plovers.

Eventually, the route heads down to meet the Maize Beck **K**, GPS 54° 38.142 02° 21.114, which is soon crossed by a footbridge **L**, GPS 54° 38.151 02° 21.814. The path follows an old miners' route, going gradually uphill, to High Cup, **M**. (This is a sensitive landscape so try to avoid shortcuts.) Head west-south-west up the path to High Cup Plain **N**. The path is slightly vague again, but stay

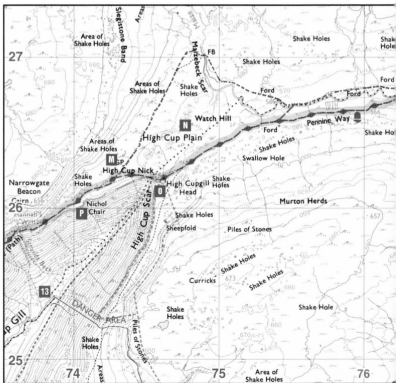

Contours are given in metres
The vertical interval is 10m

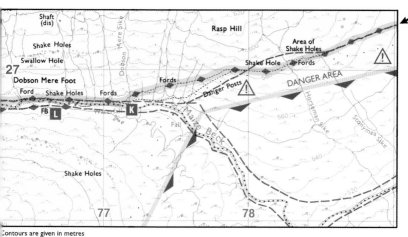

Contours are given in metres
The vertical interval is 10m

in the same direction, watch for stone markers and turn right by an arrowed one to High Cupgill Head , where suddenly the floor drops away from you, becoming a terrifying, yawning chasm.

At the foot of the glaciated amphitheatre, High Cup Gill **13**, a fine silvery thread, snakes south-west to the Eden Valley. Beyond lie the Lakeland fells. This is your reward. Enjoy it.

When you get round to picking your jaw up from the floor and brushing the grass from your chin, a path bears right, around the other side of High Cup, heading south-west above a stack of rock called Nichol Chair **P**. If you're in luck or running a bit late, you may even get the sun setting into the Lakeland hills in front of you. Another photo opportunity?

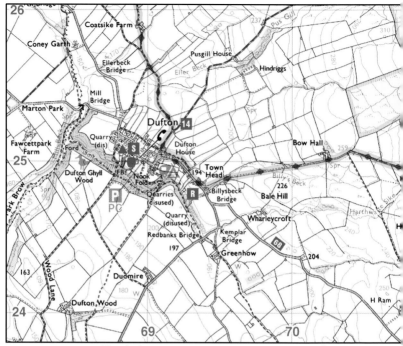

3 km or 2 miles   Contours are given in metre

Cairns mark the rocky downhill path at first, before it drops down to an old drove road **Q**, which leads directly to the village of **Dufton 14**. This is another descent that seems to go on for ever, in the shadow of perky, conical Dufton Pike on your right. Green rolling pastures, cobwebbed by drystone walls and hedgerows of blackthorn and gooseberry, soften the roadside as it reaches Town Head **R**.

The Way turns right along the main road towards the village before turning north close to the Methodist church and on to Dufton's lovely village green **S**.

What a day, eh? Now try and get a good night's sleep. You'll need it . . .

Public transport

Holwick (0.5 mile/0.8 km) 🚌
Forest-in-Teesdale (1 mile/1.6 km) 🚌
Langdon Beck (0.3 mile/0.5 km) 🚌
Dufton (on route) 🚌

Refreshments, public toilets and information

Holwick (0.5 mile/0.8 km)
🚻 Strathmore Arms
Langdon Beck (0.3 mile/0.5 km) 🚻
Langdon Beck Hotel

Dufton (on route) 🚻
Food shops: Forest-in-Teesdale

Accommodation

Holwick (0.5 mile/0.8 km) Low Farm Way hostel, camping
High Force (on route) High Force Hotel
Forest-in-Teesdale (1 mile/1.6 km) The Dale
Langdon Beck (0.3 mile/0.6 km) The Dale, East Underhurth Farm, Langdon Beck Hotel, Langdon Beck Hostel
Dufton (on route) wide selection

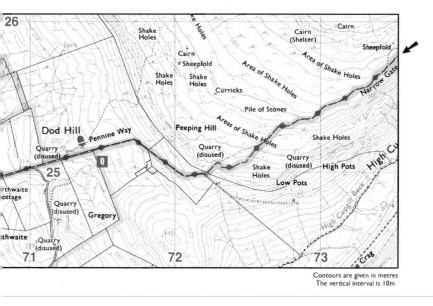

Contours are given in metres
The vertical interval is 10m

Thief! A glacier has made off with the floor.
To many, High Cup is the highlight of the Way.

▮▮ Dufton to Alston

via Great Dun Fell, Cross Fell and Garrigill
20 miles (32 km)

Ascent 3,410 feet (1,040 metres)
Descent 3,085 feet (940 metres)
Highest point Cross Fell: 2,930 feet (893 metres)
Lowest point Dufton: 590 feet (180 metres)

There's no gentle way to break it to you: today is the toughest day on the Pennine Way. It's the longest leg, it includes the highest point and more than 3,000 feet (1,000 metres) of ascent, up to the loftiest ground in England outside the Lake District. Plus route-finding can be tricky and some sections are exposed. Today may well be a thorough test of equipment (waterproofs and a working compass essential), fitness, navigation skills and your outdoor mentality. It's the sort of day where, if the weather forecast is foul (and talking of weather, England's coldest temperature and strongest wind gust were recorded here), a rest day wouldn't be too cowardly an idea.

If neither time nor weather is on your side, you could take the road up to Great Dun Fell, skipping Knock Fell and a section of difficult moorland. In good weather, however, it's a day of stunning views (apparently – few can verify this) and classic Way experiences. Either way, it's likely this section will be first on the reminiscence list in Kirk Yetholm's Border Hotel. This is how you earn your Wayfarer spurs.

A long climb gets you to the high fells, then continues over three summits, including the notorious Cross Fell, where navigation requires alertness even in friendly weather. The long descent to Garrigill, down the endless Corpse Road miners' track, is almost as notorious as Cross Fell, but at least navigation is simple. Some may wish to call it a day in Garrigill; otherwise you follow the South Tyne into Alston. It's mostly flat walking and route-finding is sometimes fiddly through fields.

There are are no facilities between Dufton and Garrigill, though Greg's Hut, an excellent walkers' bothy and a Way institution, offers shelter and the potential for an overnight stop.

As the fells here were mined, straying far from the path could be dangerous. In less ominous news, you'll also notice you're now in the land of burns, not becks.

Things to look out for

▮ **The Helm Wind** Nowhere else in Britain has a wind with its own name, and conditions have to be just right to create it. A north-easterly wind rises with the landscape, which on the eastern side of the Pennines is a long, gentle slope. But a higher, warmer layer of wind acts like a glass ceiling, squeezing the air through a small gap at the top of the ridge. The wind, not the least bit pleased by all the inconvenience, charges down the steep slope of the western Pennines into the Eden Valley, picking up ferocious speed, then it curls back up, creating a distinctive rolling cloud (the 'helm', as in helmet). You know the wind is in residence when there are two parallel, apparently stationary, clouds above the Pennines. One local has said it sent Brussels sprouts ricocheting round his garden like machine-gun bullets. Others have lost stone barns. The wind can rumble around for hours or days and is more likely in winter and spring. As if today didn't have enough against you already . . .

■ **Mining speak** Though there's no lead mining in the Pennines today, the hills have been plundered for their natural resources (especially lead, for roofs) since the Romans. Mining ruins can be seen around Keld and Alston, but it's around Dufton that names on the map more obviously bear the legacy of the area's industrial past. Today's route reveals a jumble of strange words, such as 'hushes' – gashes in hillsides where dams were constructed across natural clefts and water was released to scour the vegetation and uncover mineral deposits, making the natural channel much larger. Other mining jargon includes 'shake hole' – a conical depression in the ground caused by underground subsidence. While we're on the subject, the word 'cairn', now universally known as a pile of stones used as a waymarker, once referred to a mound of stones over an ancient burial site.

5 Great Dun Fell A giant golf ball on the summit means the Pennine's second-highest hill is unlikely to gain any fans, and predictably Wainwright despised it. 'There is no other (hill) so debased, so abused,' he wrote. 'A monstrous miscellany of paraphernalia . . . disgraces it . . . quite the ugliest of all summits.' While it sure looks ugly, the prominent radar station means no one will get lost trying to find Great Dun Fell in anything short of white-out conditions, and aviation is much safer for its presence. Plus we know more about the weather. In fact, the UK's strongest-ever wind gust was recorded here. Tarmac enthusiasts may wish to know that the road to the summit of Great Dun Fell is the highest in England.

So that's what Cross Fell looks like. One of the most elusive views on the Way.

6 Cross Fell Some places along the Pennine Way don't live up to their fearsome reputations. But Cross Fell does. The highest point in England outside the Lake District is also the coldest place in the country, according to the Met Office. Wainwright called it 'a surly beast, often in a black mood', and in 1747 the *Gentlemen's Magazine* said Cross Fell is 'generally ten months buried in snow and eleven in clouds'. It'll be little comfort to know it probably got its moniker because a cross was erected here by St Augustine to drive away devils (which doesn't seem to have worked). Or that before that it may have been called 'Fiend's Fell', presumably because of the Helm Wind. A week after I was here a walker called out mountain rescue after getting lost on Cross Fell's summit. That said, on a clear day summit views are magnificent, Wainwright labelling them the finest on the entire Pennine Way. The acidic flushes around here produce several obscure plants, including alpine foxtail grass.

11 Greg's Hut This bothy (an emergency overnight hut) can be a very welcome sight and is something of a Pennine Way institution. The former lead-mining hut is named after John Gregory, who died in a mountaineering accident in the Alps in 1968. There are two rooms, tables, chairs, a sleeping platform, a fireplace and, if your luck's in, firewood supplied by the saintly people of Greg's Hut Society. It's a good lunch spot, a very welcome shelter in bellicose conditions, or even a night stop (which one waterlogged guidebook writer took advantage of). As ever in this sort of place, the visitors' book is full of humour and stories – don't forget to add yours. There's always someone who's had a worse time than you.

12 Garrigill After the high, wet fells, some may want to kiss the little village of Garrigill when they see it. Wainwright talked of its 'verdant loveliness' and even in a downpour it looks perfectly attractive. The name is derived from Gerard's Gill – *gill* being an Old Norse word for a narrow valley. Like Dufton, the village is clustered around a picturesque green, there are some accommodation options and the post office (on the right just before the green) sells supplies and even pots of tea (though they'll send you round to the church porch to drink it).

13 Alston The narrow, cobbled streets that cling to the hillside claim to belong to the highest market town in England. While that may be disputed, there's no arguing Alston's history or charm. The quaint Market Cross, its signature building, dates from 1765, though runaway lorries have twice demolished it. Few places along the Pennine Way have as many facilities as Alston, including banks, medium-sized supermarkets and plenty of accommodation, so it's a good time to replenish stocks.

The tellingly named Corpse Road goes on for what feels like a lifetime. Though it's also a handy navigational aid.

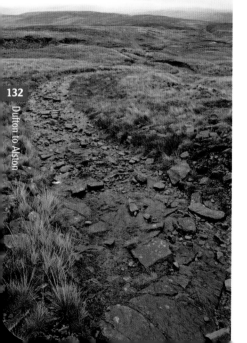

Dufton to Alston

Route description

Leave the main road in Dufton close to the Methodist church **A**, beside a cottage with the inscription 'LWONIN FYEAT 1648' above the door. (The owner explained the words are the local dialect for 'Lane Foot' – most likely meaning footpath.)

Follow the hawthorn-lined track, then after a dip turn left through a gate and on to a flagstone path that goes between fields. The path becomes a track, then goes through Coatsike Farm **B** while all the time the curious and conical Dufton Pike watches you from the right.

You're soon on Hurning Lane, which was once used by lead miners. Halsteads **C**, GPS 54° 38.243 02° 28.797, the next

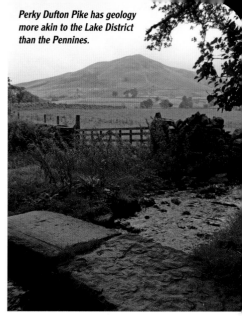

Perky Dufton Pike has geology more akin to the Lake District than the Pennines.

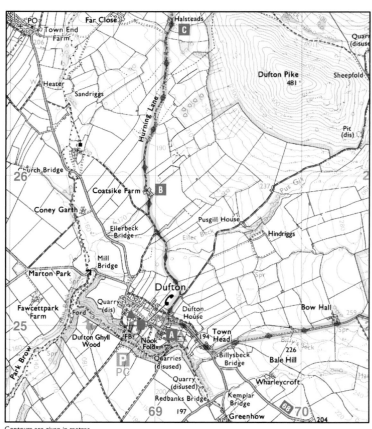

Contours are given in metres
The vertical interval is 10m

farm, is deserted and the Way contours around Cosca Hill. There's a lovely view back from here, across the Eden Valley to the Lakeland fells. Make the most of it: the atmosphere's about to change, as the gentle lowlands morph into rough pasture and foreboding moorland.

Great Rundale Beck is crossed at an old clapper bridge 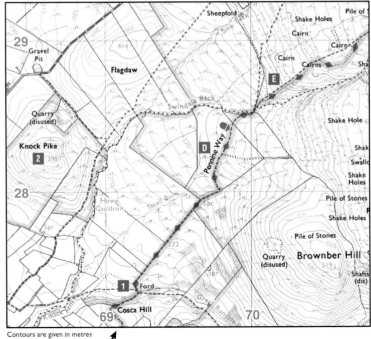, the stone slabs worn smooth by the feet of shepherds, miners and long-distance walkers. Away to the left is conical Knock Pike **2** which, like Dufton Pike, looks like a Pennine outlaw. Indeed these hills have more in common geologically with the northern Lake District, being composed of Skiddaw slate.

On the lower slopes of Scald Fell the Way bears left **D**, GPS 54° 38.904 02° 28.169, continuing north as the track turns east. If the weather's half-decent, ahead you'll see Cross Fell and Great Dun Fell – the latter with the large golf ball-style radar installation on its summit.

After crossing a footbridge over Swindale Beck, climb sharply, taking a direct line north-east along an indistinct but cairned path **E**, GPS 54° 39.092 02° 27.917. You enter the massive Moor House Upper Teesdale reserve again, as you continue up, parallel to a steep-sided cleft on your right.

The next 1.25 miles (2 km) are steady climbing, following posts, stone markers, cairns and an old hush. The ascent leads past a stone wind shelter, GPS 54° 39.425 02° 26.920, then to Knock Old Man **3**, GPS 54° 39.903 02° 26.123, which is an obelisk of stones on the brow of Knock Fell (the highest point on the Way so far, though there's plenty more uphill to come). Carry on up, to reach the cairned summit of Knock Fell **F**, GPS 54° 39.989 02° 26.008.

In bad weather route-finding is tricky and getting the compass out would be wise. The Way angles north-west as it begins to drop downhill, but twice the path seems to disappear into a scattering of stones. At the first carry straight on; at the second look for

Dufton to Alston

Contours are given in metres
The vertical interval is 10m

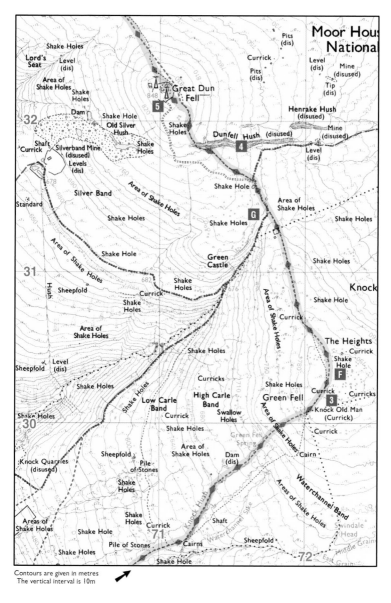

Contours are given in metres
The vertical interval is 10m

a cairn, GPS 54° 40.146 02° 26.069, and angle slightly left of it and you should see the very welcome sight of flagstones, GPS 54° 40.171 02° 26.096, even if they can be slippy.

At the tarmac road G, GPS 54° 40.619 02° 26.386, which leads to Great Dun

Fell's radar station, go right and follow it for a short distance. Then leave it to the right, GPS 54° 40.721 02° 26.484, by a signpost. The Way swerves left to avoid Dunfell Hush 4, then passes over the summit of Great Dun Fell 5 to the right of the radar station.

The Cross Fell range can look deceptively green and friendly from down below, but don't fall for its tricks.

In clear weather Cross Fell dominates the skyline (apparently), but Little Dun Fell becomes visible in the foreground. The Way heads directly for it, downhill on a stone-slabbed path to a marshy saddle , then climbing to the open summit.

From the scattering of boulders and a stone wind-shelter, the Way descends again to another saddle and past the head of the Tees as the route goes steadily up a mainly stone-slabbed path , heading straight up to Cross Fell's summit plateau .

If the weather's hostile, it's worth knowing that the first large cairn , GPS 54° 42.062 02°28.505, isn't the top (sigh . . .); nor is the second large cairn, GPS 54° 42.157 02°28.817 (groan). The summit proper of Cross Fell has both a triangulation point (at a height of 2,930 feet/893 metres), GPS 54° 42.182 02°29.088, and a cross-shaped, stone wind-shelter (like Great Shunner Fell's).

The summit is sometimes visited by mountain birds such as the dotterel. You'll doubtless have your own opinion of Cross Fell, and that will be largely determined by the weather (which is the nice way of saying its name is a swear word to some guidebook writers). The good news is you've made it to the highest point of both the Pennines and the Pennine Way. The bad news? It's taken two-thirds of the day to get one-third of the distance. But the rest of this section is much easier.

From the shelter, change direction to head north-north-west, from cairn to cairn, and descend via Crossfell Well towards a well-worn track . The views to the north are apocalyptically bleak. It's glorious stuff.

The Way turns right to follow the track **10** – the discouragingly named Corpse Road, which will take you all the way to Garrigill several miles away.

The old miners' track is so named because villagers from Garrigill took their dead this way to the nearest consecrated ground, in Kirkland, rather than because Wayfarers often breathe their last here, though that mightn't seem too improbable by this stage of your day. Though it's a hard, knobbly walking surface, it will be a welcome change (at first), navigationally at least, after the uncertainty of the high moors. There are old mine works around, so be careful about straying off-track.

Go past **Greg's Hut** **11**, GPS 54° 42.771 02°28.787, and several miles later, after

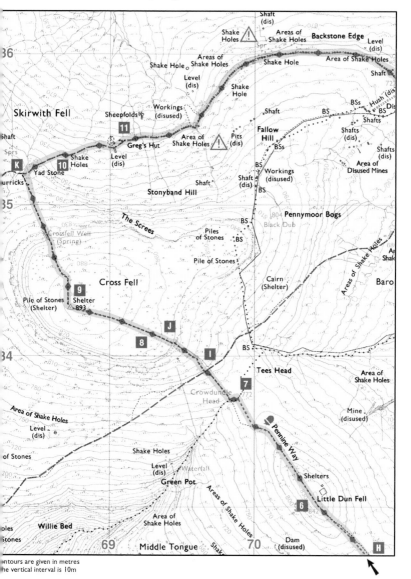

Contours are given in metres
The vertical interval is 10m

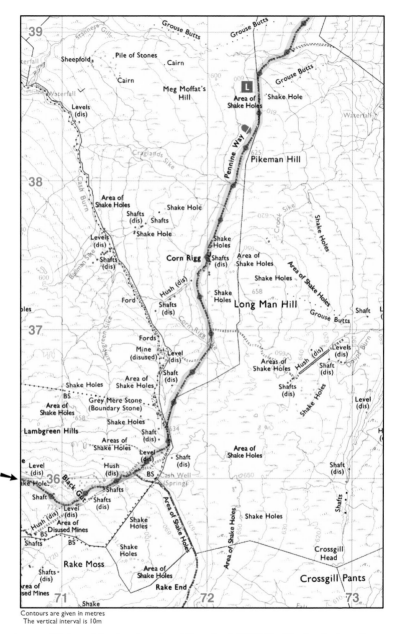

Contours are given in metres
The vertical interval is 10m

a gate **L**, bear right, then drop downhill to meet a wall **M**. Go through another gate **N**, which takes you on to a walled lane to descend steeply past a Methodist chapel **O** and left along the road into Garrigill **12**. The Way heads along the main street and, once out of the village, where the road bears uphill to the left, a stile **P** leads right and parallel to the South Tyne.

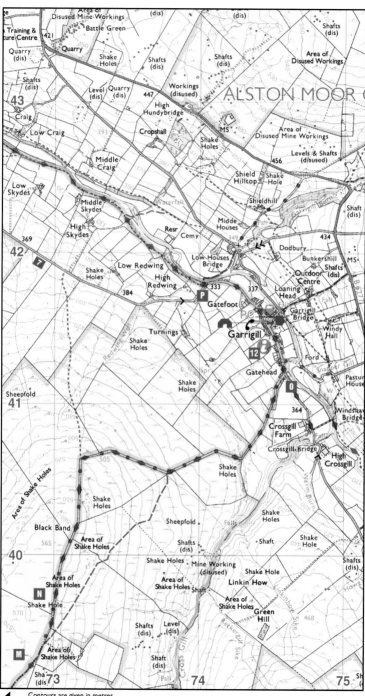

Contours are given in metres
The vertical interval is 10m

Eventually you cross the river at a footbridge **Q** and continue along the north bank, until you come to a signpost where you bear right **R** and go obliquely uphill (ignore a track on the right at crest) to Bleagate Farm **S**. Turn left and go through the farm, then turn immediately right in the first field to switch north and continue ahead.

The Way follows a line well above the river, mostly over pasture, so the walk into Alston **13** is completed along a firm, well-signed and well-trodden path above a steep tree-shaded bank. You'll soon see the youth hostel on the right. Alternatively, keep straight on for town. If you're continuing on the Way, take the next left, downhill to the road.

Public transport
Alston (on route) 🚌 🚐

Refreshments, public toilets and information
Garrigill ☕, post office
Alston (on route) ☕, 🍴 wide selection
Food shops: Garrigill, Alston

Public toilets: Garrigill, Alston
Information: Alston (Tourist Information 01434 382244)

Accommodation
Garrigill (on route) Garrigill Post Office Guesthouse, Bridge View B&B, East View
Alston (on route) wide selection

The historic village of Alston – a welcome sight at the end of the day.

Dufton to Alston

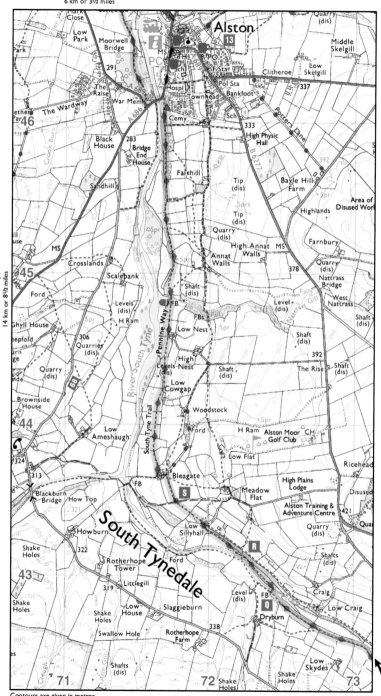

Contours are given in metres
The vertical interval is 10m

12 Alston to Greenhead

through Slaggyford and over Blenkinsopp Common
16.5 miles (26 km)

Ascent 1,770 feet (540 metres)
Descent 2,295 feet (700 metres)
Highest point Whitley Castle: 1,050 feet (320 metres)
Lowest point Greenhead: 492 feet (150 metres)

Today is unlikely to be in anyone's Pennine Way Top Five. Or Top Ten. Or even Fifteen. In fact, it could be your least favourite day.

Wainwright labelled the section after the B6292 tedious, dull and complicated. 'If the remainder of the Pennine Way was like this (happily it isn't), here would be the place to pack it in and go home.' It's not genuinely awful, just a bit, well, boring, really. Plus route-finding is fiddly. But then we have been rather spoilt recently.

Sadly, today marks the end of Pennines, at Round Hill and Wain Rigg. The day starts off following a former railway line (now the South Tyne Trail), ducking under viaducts, before joining the Maiden Way, going over Hartley Burn floodplain and the soggy wilderness of Blenkinsopp Common. The Way zigzags between fields, farms, walls, bridges and bogs, so you'll want to keep this guidebook and its excellent maps close (as you should always, of course).

The day's prominent noise will be squelching, and if you meet a Wayfarer with dry feet in Greenhead you'll know they cheated and caught a cab.

However, today does end at the stirring Hadrian's Wall and the next few days have many treats in store; it just requires this linking section to get there. And you are in the great outdoors – things could be worse.

Unusually, today some signs seem to favour wayfarers going north–south, and it's sometimes worth having a peek round the other side of the wall for a half-hidden sign, even if the arrow is pointing the 'wrong' way. There's also nowhere for lunch after Knarsdale, which has a pub (whoop).

Things to look out for

2 5 Whitley Castle and the Maiden Way
Built to defend a road linking the Stanegate at Carvoran with Watling Street at Kirkby Thore, this is the highest stone-built Roman fort in Britain. It's nearly 9 acres of earthworks; ramparts and ditches and a large flat platform in the centre. Drystone walls cut straight across the fort as if it were not there. For centuries farmers, and the rest of society, showed a flagrant disdain for history and apparently worthless relics. The Romans were our invaders after all. There are more Roman connections today, as the Way goes along the Maiden Way for a time.

This thoroughfare was probably laid in about AD 80, when Agricola blazed a trail northwards to crush those pesky barbarians, after conquering the rest of Britain.

█ **Viaducts** You'll pass several viaducts today. Nine were built to carry the Alston branch of the Newcastle–Carlisle railway in the early 1850s. The trains mainly transported lead ore from the local mines to Haltwhistle, but by the 1880s production

had slumped. Coal from the Tindale Fell Colliery kept things ticking over, but the line closed in 1976. The section between Alston and Kirkhaugh, however, has re-opened as a narrow-gauge steam line for tourists and some of the viaducts have a new use. The five-arched viaduct near Lintley Farm is home to pipistrelle and long-eared bats, while the nearby trees are the territory of the bigger noctule bat.

Route description

At the edge of Alston, cross the A686 road bridge **A** to find the Pennine Way signposted just after the road turns right **B**. The Way begins as a track, turning into a narrow path with the river and town to the right. The path continues along the edge of a pasture through the old gates of Harbut Lodge **C**. Go to the left of the Harbut Lodge buildings, across

a small field and over a step-stile on to a track **D**. The track leads up to the A689 and you turn right along it, briefly, before veering left across a marshy field and through a gate to the right of an old barn **1**. White paint around the byre door was to help cattle, and bleary-eyed milkmaids, find their way in at pre-dawn milking time.

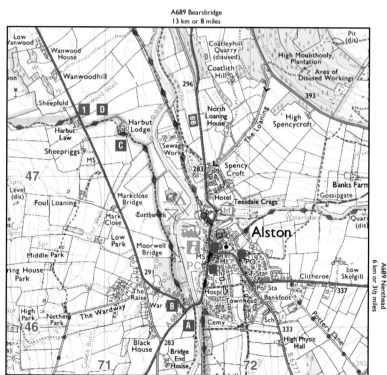

A689 Bearsbridge
13 km or 8 miles

Contours are given in metres
The vertical interval is 10m

Kirkhaugh Station on the South Tynedale Railway, which follows part of the route of the old Haltwhistle to Alston branch line.

Just after the gate there is a little stream or sike, home to brooklime, a kind of speedwell with little blue flowers. Beyond the stream the Way heads uphill over pasture, leading to a ladder-stile over a wall **E**, GPS 54° 49.225 02° 27.824. Cross the marshy pasture to the north-west, then the Way drops down to the footbridge **F** and enters Northumberland.

From here the route climbs up a very muddy path, crossing a stile and heading uphill to meet a track **G**, GPS N54 49.704 W2 28.462. Bear left (north-west) through pasture and out on to the open fells. Follow the track, which is a little vague, arcing to the right and around the grassy ramparts of Whitley Castle **2**. Climb a ladder-stile over a wall and follow the wall down to Castle Nook **H**, where the path crosses a stream, heading down to the road. Cross the road, go through a gate and take a path on the right side of a wall which leads to Dyke House **I**, at which the route clips the corner of an enclosure around some houses.

Navigating these fields is fiddly. However, from here to Lintley Farm, as long as you've got the road to your left and the South Tynedale railway to your right, you can't get properly lost.

The Way continues north-north-west with a wall to the left. At a gate where the wall ends **J**, the route is obscure but goes straight on, across rough grassland to Kirkhaugh (*haugh* is Norse for 'flat land beside a river'), at which a tarmac track is followed left. Just after a group of buildings on the right, and before the little Wesleyan chapel **3**, the Way turns right over a cattlegrid and heads straight on into a field. Continue heading north-north-west, roughly in a straight line, across fields and stiles, keeping parallel to the train track and heading just to the left of the bridge below Lintley Farm **K**. The path drops to cross a footbridge over Thornhope Burn and under the viaduct **4**. The Way bears north-east around a field and down to meet the South Tyne again. But at the

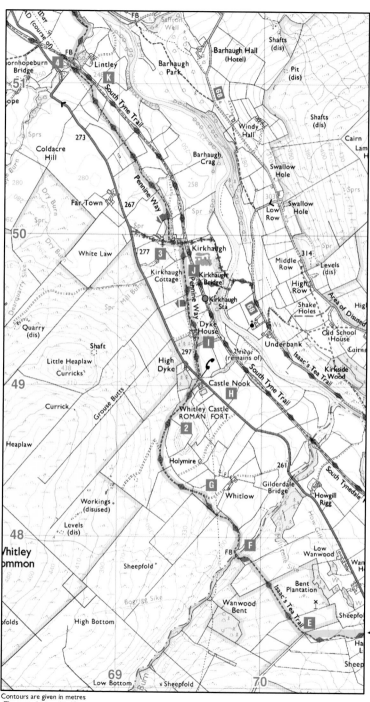

Contours are given in metres
The vertical interval is 10m

next bridge **L** the Way bids the river farewell and bears left to a road, which you follow. The A689 follows the old track of the **Maiden Way** **5** and leads into the village of Slaggyford **6** ('slaggy' means 'muddy', which will be no surprise by now).

In Slaggyford, take the first road on the left, uphill towards the Yew Tree Chapel, a B&B and another former Methodist chapel. The Way leads down a track to its right **M**, GPS 54° 48.536 02° 26.510.

You'll pass under hawthorn and ash trees, then willow, signifying wet ground, then later birch and hazel, as the path gets drier. Ignore the track turning on to the stone bridge on the left and give the

same treatment to another left turn after a small wooden bridge, before the path drops down to the Knar Burn and a footbridge, with a good view of another viaduct **7**. Turn right after crossing it and bear left to go under an old railway bridge, GPS 54° 52.221 02° 30.699, and continue along a track to Merry Knowe **N**, where you need to head right and go over three stone stiles to get around the buildings (it's more troublesome than Cross Fell!).

The Way crosses a wall at another stile and heads over pastureland, then crosses a road and makes its way over pasture again towards another viaduct **8**. Just before this a path bears right down to a

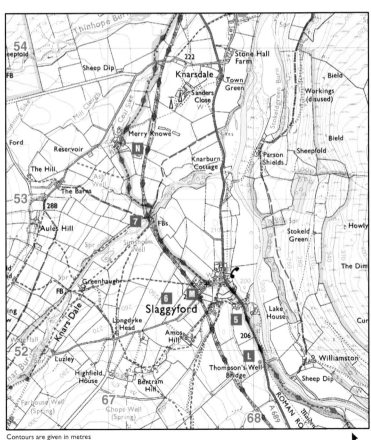

Contours are given in metres
The vertical interval is 10m

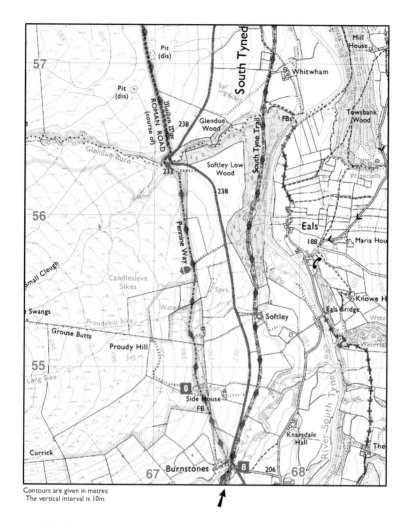

Contours are given in metres
The vertical interval is 10m

road, which is followed left across the Thinhope Burn **0**. Follow signs through a gate and uphill to a track that takes you, at last, to open moorland. The views look even better than normal thanks to all that yucky fieldwork.

Glendue Fell is to the left, while north-east, across the wooded South Tyne Valley, Wallace's Crags stand out on Ashholme Common. To the south is (talk of the devil) the Cross Fell range. Underfoot is the Maiden Way, well-defined and carrying you in the footsteps of Agricola and his army.

The Way leaves the track to the right but keeps to the very edge of the moorland (ignore a track that goes uphill to the left just after you've passed a barn on your right) and soon drops down to cross the pretty Glendue Burn. Feet still dry? They won't be for long.

The Way quickly rises again to cross a wall and travels along the moor edge of Lambley Common beside the Maiden Way. Grouse, curlews and golden plovers are abundant here, while there's a chance of seeing merlins and other birds of prey.

The moors beckon you ever onwards . . . (Ever get the idea Kirk Yetholm doesn't really exist?)

Over the road, follow the wall to meet intermittent stone flags over boggy ground. Make for a grassy knoll, then a stile and wooden posts mark the way as you continue north-north-west to High House 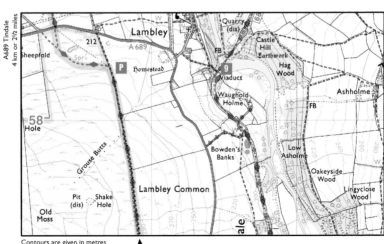 **Q**, a Top Withins-esque ruined barn, GPS 54° 55.946 02° 31.815, on a hill.

Descend along a grassy spur to cross Hartley Burn at the bridge and turn left along the burn's side, before following the fence uphill, past a stile warning you it's 'NOT Pennine Way'. The path continues across farmland from stile to stile, past the steading of Batey Shield, then down to the footbridge over Kellah Burn and a side road, and up a track to Greenriggs.

Go through the gate to the left of the house **R**, over a stile, then the Way climbs approximately straight up the middle of the field (where the path is hard to detect) to a ladder-stile **S**, GPS 54° 56.897 02° 32.606, before releasing you on to a featureless block of boggy moorland. This is Hartleyburn Common, leading to Blenkinsopp Common, a soggy and silent wasteland of hair-moss and coarse grasses. It's a lonely place (I loved it). Walk north-west, aiming to the left of the brow of Round Hill **T** and a fence-line to the west. When you reach it bear right, north, for 1.5 miles (2.4 km)

Lambley, with its nine-arched viaduct **9**, lies in the valley to the north-east, as does the faithful ridge of the Whin Sill, last seen in Teesdale.

The wall is replaced by a fence, allowing you to enjoy a beautiful stretch of purple heather in September. The Way finally crosses the fence by a signpost (ignore the first two stiles) and starts to descend **P** towards the A689. The path becomes unclear though, so aim for the road and an old barn to find a Pennine Way signpost.

Contours are given in metres
The vertical interval is 10m

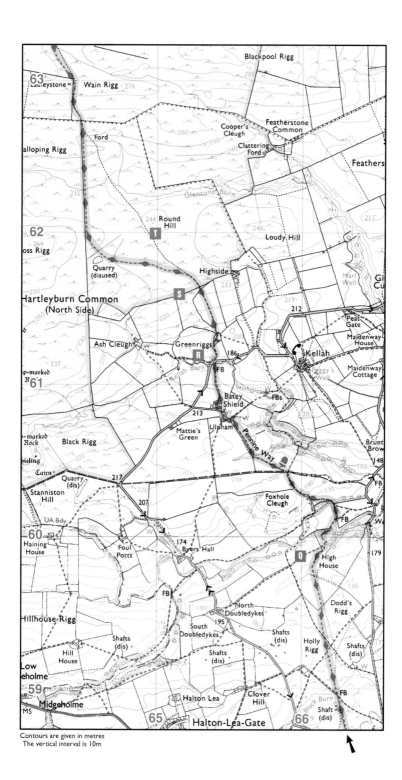

Alston to Greenhead

across rolling ground. There are lovely views back from the false summit before Black Hill. Eventually a triangulation point appears on the skyline of Black Hill ∪. Make for a point to the right of this, GPS 54° 57.937 02° 33.609, and cross the wall. The route isn't clear at all, so follow the wettest and muddiest bits, heading straight across the plateau at first, then angling left towards the stile when the ground starts to slope downwards. The busy A69 Tyne–Carlisle road, which the Way will cross, soon becomes visible below and you may be able to make out Hadrian's Wall in the distance.

In a field with a pylon and two old buildings, the path is unclear again, so aim for the bottom-right corner. Then turn right to join a track going south-east and, though it looks tempting, don't leave it till a PW sign tells you to, by some old mine workings ∨. The Way heads left, downhill and over a stile, then back under some pylons before going left at a fork to meet the road, 0.5 mile (0.8 km) west of Greenhead village ⑩.

Cross the road (without underestimating the speed of the cars, as one guidebook writer almost did) and follow it into Greenhead. Though if you're the type who feels they must step on every yard of the Way, or prefers a greener and quieter if slightly longer route into the village, you might want to continue on (see start of tomorrow's chapter).

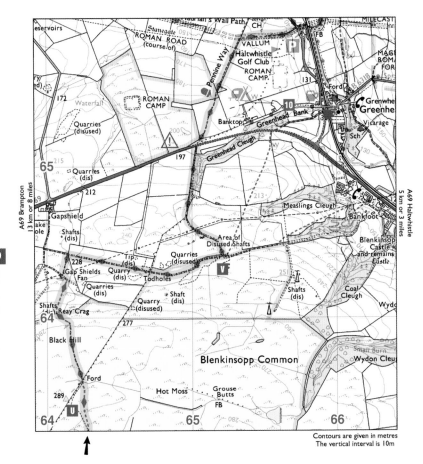

Contours are given in metres
The vertical interval is 10m

Hartleyburn Common: No tarmac. No bricks. No engines. Just lots and lots of lovely soggy moor . . .

Public transport
Greenhead (on route)

Refreshments, public toilets and information
Knarsdale (0.7 mile/1.1 km) pub Kirkstyle Inn
Greenhead (on route) wide selection

Food shops: Greenhead
Toilets: Greenhead

Accommodation
Slaggyford (on route) Yew Tree Chapel
Knarsdale (0.7 mile/1.1 km) Stonehall Farm, Stonecroft B&B
Greenhead (on route) wide selection

13 Greenhead to Bellingham

via Hadrian's Wall, Wark Forest and Shitlington Crag
22 miles (35 km)

Ascent 3,051 feet (930 metres)

Descent 3,117 feet (950 metres)

Highest point Windshields Crag: 1,132 feet (345 metres)

Lowest point Bellingham: 392 feet (119 metres)

While today your eyes are in for a visual treat and your mind's in for a historical treat, your calves are in for . . . the opposite of treat. There are a lot of ups and downs today along Hadrian's Wall – the third most ascent of a Pennine Way day (after Cross Fell and the first day). On the plus side, your toes mightn't get wet until the afternoon.

Today is another Pennine Way classic. It follows the Wall for 8 glorious miles (12.8 km), including its most dramatic stretches. It's thrilling to walk in the footsteps of Roman soldiers and there are magnificent views to match. Wainwright thought the Pennine Way should end here, with Hadrian's Wall providing a wonderful climax.

This is a long day and it feels it. Plus there's the culture shock of suddenly walking with lots of people, some of them wearing clean clothes, as the Way briefly teams up with Hadrian's Wall Path (for which Aurum Press also supply the official Trail Guide).

At Rapishaw Gap you break from the stones and crowds towards the silent Wark Forest, then farmland and a little bit of moor. The day's finale, along the road to Bellingham, is torturous and will be a favourite for the Worst End To A Day's Walk On The Way award.

The first half is a doddle for route-finding. Later on the fields and farms can be fiddly, but at least they lack the incessant ups and downs.

The only facilities involve a detour to the wonderfully named Once Brewed, which is really only a pub and youth hostel, or a stop at a friendly farm late on.

You could treat yourself to a shorter day here, leisurely enjoying the Wall and staying in Once Brewed. Indeed, the most famous Hadrian's Wall view, towards Cuddy's Crags, and the finest excavated fort, at Housesteads (Vercovicium), are about 1 mile (1.6 km) off route. Other options include a campsite at Stonehaugh, about 8 miles (12.8 km) south of Bellingham, and a B&B at Hetherington, 2 miles (3.2 km) further on.

Things to look out for

2 Thirlwall Castle This ruin of a fortified tower-house, dating back nearly 700 years, is only yards from the Way and worth a quick nose-about. Thirl-Wall means 'gap in the wall' in Olde English speak and probably referred to a break in Hadrian's Wall. The castle was built from stone taken from the Wall and the Roman fort of Carvoran. It's by Thirlwall Castle that Caledonian tribesmen are thought to have broken through Roman lines during the Barbarian Conspiracy of 367.

6 Hadrian's Wall 'No sight in England is more impressive than the Roman Wall,' wrote Christopher Wright in his 1967 Pennine Way guidebook. The Way follows the Wall for 8 miles (12.8 km) along the crest of Whin Sill, though the stonework once snaked across England for a full 73 miles (117 km) – or 80 Roman miles. It's a masterpiece of military engineering and one of the finest Roman remnants in Europe. The Wall's original construction took eight years, starting in AD 122, and was supervised by the Emperor Hadrian, who'd seen barricades of turf work effectively while fighting in Germany. The reason for its construction is still debated by historians, but the threat of pesky war-mongering Scots is the most likely factor. Stretches of it are still intact, others have been restored. The Cawfields–Walltown Quarry section is widely acknowledged as the most dramatic part – and it's on the Way. Housesteads Fort (Vercovicium), the best-preserved army base, is about 1 mile (1.6 km) off the Way and 'a highlight too interesting to miss', according to Wainwright.

19 Comyn's Cross After Wark Forest you cross a stretch of moorland before re-entering the forest (see page 159), and a little to the east there's a standing stone called Comyn's Cross. Legend has it that the sons of King Arthur heard their father had given a gold cup to a local chieftain, Comyn (or Cumming). They rode forth to retrieve the gift and slew the chieftain here, which does on the face of it seem a little bit harsh. You'd like to think they at least asked nicely for it back first.

Farming history Farm fans will be cockahoop today. The latter half of the day involves navigating around several farms, many of them centuries old. The most intriguing is Lowstead, where the house and adjoining byre are bastel-houses dating back to the 16th century and the walls are 4 feet (1.2 metres) thick. The little yard has more byres and a cart shed and granary. Horneystead Farm dates back to 1837 and is next to the ruin of a

fortified bastel-house built about 1600. Nearby, The Ash is 18th–19th century, with an elaborate Victorian conservatory or porch. Leadgate is of similar vintage. A little further on, the hilly pasture on either side of the road, marked on the map as a 'homestead', was a typical Romano-British settlement: a rectangular enclosure and several circular stone huts. A mosaic of field systems used to provide barley for the Wall forts' occupying garrison.

Border Forest Today you enter Wark Forest, the southern part of Kielder Forest, the largest man-made woodland in Europe. Conifer plantations are often viewed with disdain – Wainwright thought the Wark spruces were 'living the life of battery hens'. But the trees have a long history in the north and juniper and pine were once more widespread than oak here. Kielder Forest was a panic response to timber shortages after the First World War and large blocks of spruce were hastily planted irrespective of watercourses or conservation. Attitudes have changed and alder, birch and rowan trees are being planted along watercourses and footpaths, while Sites of Special Scientific Interest are managed sensitively and native broadleaf species are increasing. There are more birds and animals in an acre of forest than an acre of moorland, and red squirrels benefit from the plantations – Kielder is one of the last English strongholds – as do roe deer and foxes.

28 Bellingham Pronounced 'Bellinjum', this inviting little town has plenty of history, plus a nearby beauty spot. A 13th-century church of St Cuthbert has an unusual stone-slabbed roof, constructed centuries ago to replace previous ones burned down in Scottish raids. A track from near the centre of town follows Hareshaw Burn and goes through a car park to Hareshaw Dene, a beautiful valley clothed in ancient wych-elms and oaks, which leads to Hareshaw Linn, one of the most attractive waterfalls in the country. Stock up on cash and food here, if needs be, as there are very few facilities further north.

Route description

Just outside Greenhead, go up the steep bank and head north-east across fields and a golf course 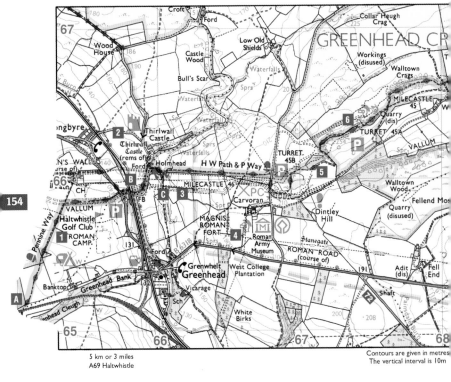 (stick to the left of it to find a small footbridge and path) and down a steep, slippery bank to meet the B6318 and a terrace of red-brick houses. The Way crosses a railway line and the Pow Charney Burn , then arcs northwards to follow the larger Tipalt Burn round a field to **Thirlwall Castle** and Duffenfoot.

In front of the castle mound turn right, down to a footbridge and across the Tipalt, through a gate to pass Holmhead . Then climb left and uphill through woodland along a walled track and into open pasture where the Way follows a wide, grassy ditch beside a wall. The ditch was part of the Roman fortifications.

It's a tough climb to the brow of the hill, where the Way enters Northumberland National Park and crosses a ladder-stile, continuing east with a wall to the right. Beyond here is the unexcavated Agricolan fort of Carvoran , beside the Roman Army Museum. Walltown Quarry is to your east – once an ugly scar, it's been transformed by the National Park Authority. On the far brow you should be able to see **Hadrian's Wall** . If the grey cliffs look familiar, it's because they are part of your old pal Whin Sill.

The Way meets a road and turns right along it, then turns left into Walltown Quarry, a picnic area with a small café, toilet and a lake. Go past it and angle left to exit the quarry via a kissing-gate. Then head left, north-west, along the

5 km or 3 miles
A69 Haltwhistle

Contours are given in metres
The vertical interval is 10m

154

top of the quarry face, directly to Hadrian's Wall. Time to sharpen your sword and do up your helmet chinstrap.

Walking eastwards takes you along the crest of the Sill with the steep scarp slope, colonised by rowan, birch and aspen, to your left and the gentle slope to the right. There are sometimes patches of wild chives along here, a rare plant possibly introduced by the Romans. After a fine turret (44B) **7**, standing up to 10 courses high, the Wall dwindles to a few fragments here and there and an ordinary drystone wall.

You could easily find yourself walking through the middle of Aesica (Great Chesters) Roman fort **8** before you know it. Then the Way drops down, past a stone cottage **D**, and over a stone stile on to the road.

Thirlwall Castle: the scene of some truly Barbaric behaviour down the years – worth the minuscule detour for a quick snoop around.

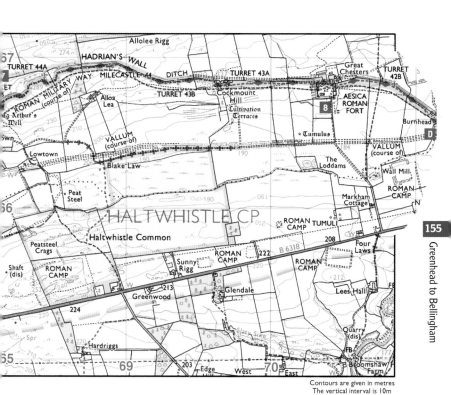

Contours are given in metres
The vertical interval is 10m

Go across the Caw Burn, then left, then right, into Cawfields Quarry , a picnic site with toilets and interpretive panels . Once past the large pond, and a cross-section of the Whin Sill , which shows the cooling pattern of the volcanic rock, a path climbs back to the ridge and passes the remains of Milecastle 42 , with a fine stretch of the *vallum* (earthwork) down to the right .

Cawfield Crags is one of the best-preserved sections of Hadrian's Wall and after Caw Gap and along Windshields Crag you reach the highest point on the Whin Sill . On a clear day from here you can see south across the Pennines to your old foe Cross Fell and north to the Cheviots (Cheviot is the whaleback to the left and, not unlike Stoodley Pike, it's going to be taunting you for a few days to come). From the triangulation point, GPS 55° 00.118 02° 24.279, at 1,132 feet (345 metres) the Way quickly descends to meet a side road , then the Steel Rigg car park .

If you're overnighting at Once Brewed, follow the Military Way to meet the side road and turn down this to the main road, known as the Military Road, or Wade's Road (because it was built by General Wade to carry troops in the 18th century).

Continuing on the main route, just before Peel Crags a gap in the Whin Sill shows the grey face of quartz-dolerite. It was cooled and weathered into near-hexagonal columns after being squeezed out as magma between beds of limestone and sandstone nearly 300 million years ago.

After Peel Crags you head down into Castle Nick and Sycamore Gap, clefts created by

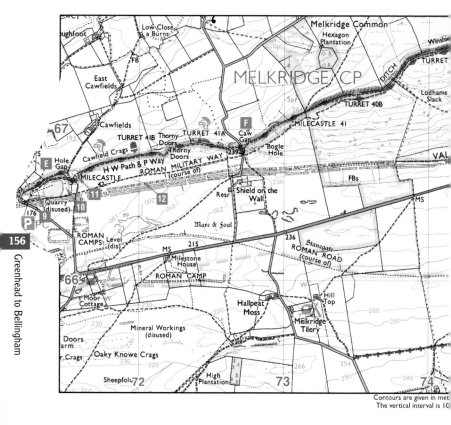

Contours are given in met
The vertical interval is 10

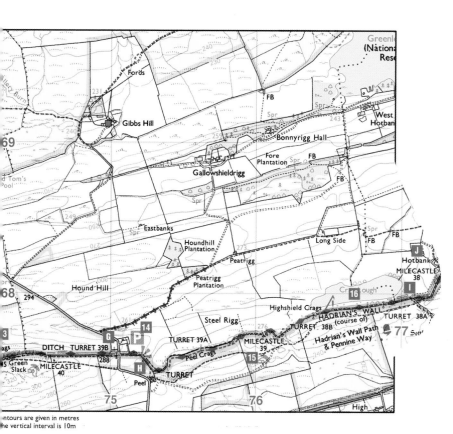

ntours are given in metres
he vertical interval is 10m

Ice Age meltwater. The loose stonework of Milecastle 39 **15** is popular with wheatears – look for a black-tipped tail and a white rump. Indeed, the name 'wheatear' has its origins in 'white-arse', but was cleaned up in Victorian times.

The view down to the Crag Lough **16** should make most people smile in appreciation. There are usually swans on the water, either whooper or mute depending on the time of year. The path drops down through a plantation of pine, wych-elm and sycamore, then leads out on to a track.

Cross it and go through a gate **I**, then up a rather mean ascent, past the grass-covered remains of Milecastle 38 and Hotbank Farm **J**, up to Hotbank

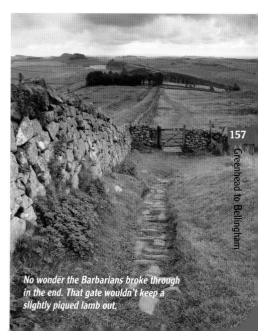

No wonder the Barbarians broke through in the end. That gate wouldn't keep a slightly piqued lamb out.

B6318 Low Brunton
14 km or 8½ km

Contours are given in metres
The vertical interval is 10m

Crags where the Wall is in good order again. At Rapishaw Gap , GPS 55°00.703 02°20.556, you can say goodbye to the crowds and those oh-so-amusing ups and downs as the Way leaves the Wall. Or carry on for a 1-mile (1.6-km) detour to the most famous Wall view, towards Cuddy's Crags, and the finest excavated fort at Housesteads (Vercovicium) **17**. Wainwright considered this 'a must', but it's still a long way to Bellingham.

Released from the Wall at a ladder-stile, take the path to the right as the Way heads north-north-east over marshy ground towards those passive-aggressive forests. Looking back and to the east the Sill rises to Sewingshields Crags, where King Arthur and his knights supposedly sleep, then drops away like a spent wave.

Over a ladder-stile, go left on to Ridley Common, which provides an unexpected interlude of some pretty stretches of purple heather in September and a pretty burn **18** all year round. The Way drops at Cragend to another burn with a footbridge

L. After a kissing-gate, go left and look for flags and posts, cross a wooden bridge then a ladder-stile, then right and briefly on to a wide track, entering Wark Forest.

To Wainwright, forest-walking in general was the antithesis of fell-walking: 'The forest is a prison, the fell is liberty.' It has its faults, but I found the trees a pleasing change.

The Way gains height steadily through the forest, along the drive. Turn right, off the track at a signpost, GPS 55° 00.118 02° 24.279, and along a path, which eventually leads out on to moorland at a step-stile and gate **M**.

Across the sea of moorgrass, make for the small group of pines **N** in a sheepfold. On this stretch I was accompanied the whole time by a massive rainbow to my left, with its pot of gold seemingly in the forest ahead of me (though I never did find it).

Take the stile leading back into the forest **O**, albeit after a possible short detour right to **Comyn's Cross** **19**, and be alert

Contours are given in metres
The vertical interval is 10m

Greenhead to Bellingham

to the possibility of forestry work and large vehicles, which may not see you on the tracks. The Way leads down, crossing four tracks, then heads east in line with Willowbog Farm , before hitting the B6320.

After a short road walk, the Way turns left along a forest track , crossing two tarmac drives, before leading out to grassy moorland by a sign promising refreshments at Horneystead Farm, 1 mile (1.6 km) further on. The Way forms the boundary of Northumberland National Park between Ladyhill Farm  and Bellingham.

Look out for posts to guide you along the next stretch (especially as wall-lines on the map don't always correspond with the wall-lines you'll see) as you bear to the left of the brow of Ground Rigg , then left down between hillocks, keeping to the upper right bank above Fawlee Sike (a 'sike' being a small stream).

If you've judged the route correctly, you should find a beautiful little waterfall  of around 20 feet (6 metres), overhung with rowan, ivy and heather, with moss-covered rocks, shelves of hart's tongue and hard fern.

From here, detour to the left to follow the line of an old dyke crossing wet drainage channels, until eventually the Way leads over a ladder-stile across a wall, then downhill with grassy dykes either side and towards the Warks Burn. A sharp right turn  through a gate and to the right of a hay barn, then left downhill, will bring you to a footbridge , GPS 55° 05.300 02° 17.695. Once on the far bank, get ready for green pastures as the route goes from farm to farm.

At Horneystead  follow signs to some very welcome refreshments on offer by a proprietress who's probably completed more long-distance treks than you. When leaving the farm, turn right, off the track, just as it bends round to the left, to go straight across the field.

Follow signs through fields past The Ash  and Lowstead  and soon after the Way follows the track eastwards , then meets a road. Tarmac is usually so unwelcome, but after hours in bogs it's a little more likeable than usual here. Follow this north-north-east, past a small quarry and limekiln on the left  and some ancient earthworks at Homestead .

Enjoy the last few bits of Hadrian's Wall as the scenery's about to change markedly (though your calfs may be pleased at that news).

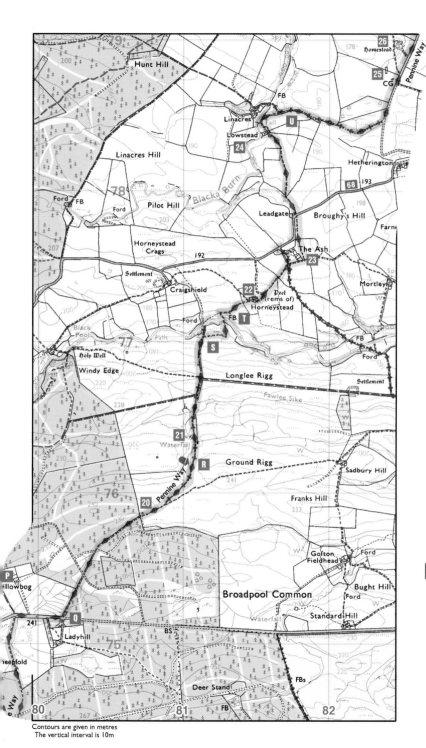

Contours are given in metres
The vertical interval is 10m

Looking back from Shitlington Crag, not far from Shitlington Hall.

Where the road meets a T-junction **V**, GPS 55° 06.424 02° 16.387, the Way continues north-east as a field path, alongside a fence. In the fourth field, head down the middle to look for a footbridge **W** hidden in the trees. Turn right on the other side, go over another bridge, then turn left through a gate, past Shitlington Hall **X**, which is only a farmhouse (Wainwright thought the name 'a trifle earthy').

The Way heads along a track, then uphill beside open pasture, before climbing up the sandstone edge of Shitlington Crag (he's not wrong, is he?), finally reaching a ladder-stile **Y** in the wall to the left, west, of the radio mast. To the south and south-west are rewarding views of the route you've just taken.

After crossing the stile and walking along a track right, eastwards, the Way suddenly heads out north-east across the rushy moorland **Z**. The path's a little unclear, so make for a marker post on the brow of the hill and carry on down into the North Tyne Valley. The views of Bellingham are reminiscent of Middleton-in-Teesdale and would round the day off nicely if it weren't for that torturous road walk still remaining.

After joining the smaller road, look for an official shortcut on the left, before joining the main road into Bellingham, where cars go dangerously fast. After crossing the bridge **27**, built in the 1830s, turn right down the steps to the park and follow the path along the river bank. Turn left past Cuddy's Well and continue into Bellingham **28** behind the town hall and into the square. Then dump your bag off and get to the pub! You've earned it today.

Public transport

Once Brewed (0.5 mile/0.8 km) 🚌🚍
Bellingham (on route) 🚌🚍

Refreshments, public toilets and information

Burnhead (on route) 🍴 Milecastle Inn
Once Brewed (0.5 mile/0.8 km) 🍴 Twice Brewed Inn
Bellingham (on route) 🍴🍺 wide selection
Food shops: Bellingham
Toilets: Walltown Quarry, Cawfields Quarry
Information: Once Brewed

(Northumberland National Park Visitor Centre, 01434 344396), Bellingham (Heritage Centre, 01434 220050)

Accommodation

Burnhead (on route) Burnhead Bed & Breakfast on Hadrian's Wall
Once Brewed (0.5 mile/0.8 km), Winchields Farm, Once Brewed YHA, Vallum Lodge, Twice Brewed Inn, Saughy Rigg Farm
Stonehaugh Stonehaugh Campsite
Hetherington Hetherington Farm
Bellingham wide selection

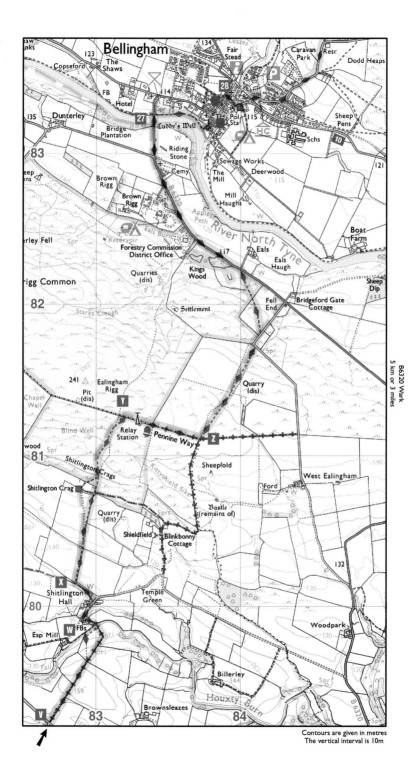

Contours are given in metres
The vertical interval is 10m

14 Bellingham to Byrness

via Whitley Pike and Brownrigg Head
15 miles (24 km)

Ascent 1,814 feet (553 metres)
Descent 1,470 feet (448 metres)
Highest point Padon Hill: 1,214 feet (370 metres)
Lowest point Bellingham: 392 feet (119 metres)

At 'only' 15 miles (24 km) this is a comparatively easy day to reach the demanding but glorious Cheviots. The section is split into two clear stages: heathery moors with wonderful views but bog-hopping skills required; and forests, which have no bogs, but few views either.

The moors come first and include some enchanting stretches of purple heather in September, but time and again you'll see your foot disappear into that squelchy, murky underworld we call bog. So the dramatic change to stony forestry track-roads is welcome, at first. But the monotonous pounding takes its toll and may have you hankering after the soft, comfortable swamps before long. It's another contender for Worst End To A Day's Walk On The Way (it got Wainwright's vote).

In the forests route-finding is a cinch, and though there are one or two blind spots on the moors, there's usually something semi-obvious to aim for. You know the score by now: if in doubt, follow the wettest, muddiest trail.

Unsurprisingly, there's nowhere to buy lunch and Byrness is barely a village. While some accommodation options supply packed lunches, meals and alcohol, there's little else here.

Things to look out for

7 Padon Hill The summit of Padon Hill bears a bell-shaped tumulus built in the 1920s and most of the stones used to build it are from the hilltop. The hill got its name from Alexander Peden, a Scottish Presbyterian who held services in places like this when Nonconformists, especially Scots, were repressed during the reign of Charles II. People attending the illicit gatherings carried a stone up the hill with them to add to the symbol of defiance.

■ Emperor moths The moorland around Padon Hill is home to Emperor moths. This beautiful creature, Britain's only member of the silk moth family, can be seen on sunny days in April and May, while the massive caterpillar, green with black bands and covered with short bristles, is seen in late summer. It feeds on heather and enjoys sunning itself on the ground, where it both intrigues and terrifies walkers.

10 Blakehopeburnhaugh The name of this farmstead has appeared in *The Guinness Book of Records* as the longest place name in England. The word is understood as: 'Blake', black; 'hope', a fertile strip of valley land; 'burn', a stream; 'haugh', low-lying land by a river. However, recent maps show neighbouring Cottonshopeburnfoot as one word where it used to be two, making it even longer.

12 Byrness The village of Byrness is a curious little settlement of terraces built by the Forestry Commission in the 1930s. It was created for workers, first to build Catcleugh Reservoir, then to plant the Border Forest. As the trees of Kielder grew, the number of foresters needed shrank, as did the hamlet. Some of the villagers evacuated from the Scottish island of St Kilda in 1930 were resettled here too. Situated just before the Cheviot traverse, Byrness is a useful stopover. Both the accommodation providers here will collect you halfway into the Cheviots, bring you back to Byrness for a second night, and return you to the Cheviots the next day.

Route description

From the centre of Bellingham follow the West Woodburn road, opposite Barclays Bank, downhill and across a bridge **A** over Hareshaw Burn. Then uphill, past the Heritage and Tourist Information Centres and out of the town, leaving the tarmac **B** to head north when the road goes east.

The Way turns through the middle of Blakelaw farmyard **C**, then angles right, up the hillside, and aims for an isolated post on the crest. Go past the corner of a wall **D**, GPS 53° 53.800 02° 03.641, and over grass-topped old coal workings. After the post, aim for the right of both a pine plantation on the skyline and an outcrop of rocks. A gate leads back on to high moorland and back into Northumberland National Park.

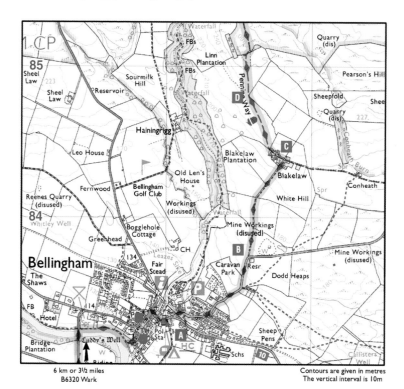

6 km or 3½ miles
B6320 Wark

Contours are given in metres
The vertical interval is 10m

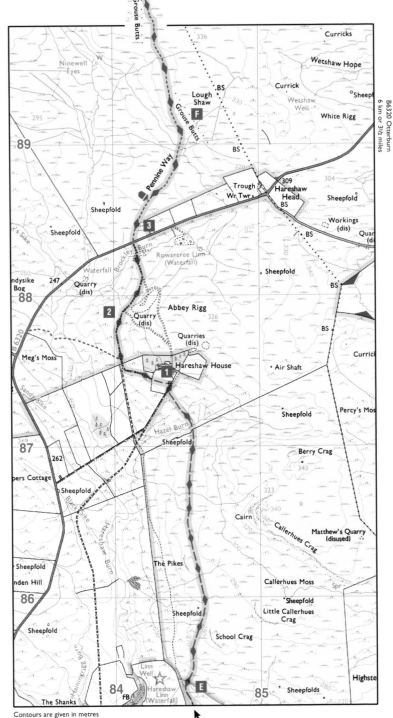

Grouse Butts

Currick

Wetshaw Hope

Ninewell
Eyes

Currick

Sheepf

Lough
Shaw

BS

Wetshaw
Well

White Rigg

F

Grouse Butts

BS

Pennine Way

BS

Trough
Wr Twr

Hareshaw
Head

309

304

BS

Sheepfold

Sheepfold

3

Sheepfold

Workings
(dis)

BS

Quar
(di

Brockley Burn

Rowantree Linn
(Waterfall)

Waterfall

ndysike
Bog

247

Quarry
(dis)

Sheepfold

BS

2

Abbey Rigg

326

Quarry
(dis)

BS

Quarries
(dis)

Meg's Moss

1 Hareshaw House

Air Shaft

Currick

Sheepfold

Percy's Mos

Hazel Burn

Berry Crag

343

87

262

rs Cottage

Sheepfold

323

340

Sheepfold

Cairn

Callerhues Crag

Matthew's Quarry
(disused)

Sheepfold

nden Hill

86

The Pikes

Callerhues Moss

Spr

Sheepfold

Little Callerhues
Crag

Sheepfold

Sheepfold

School Crag

Linn
Well

84

FB

Hareshaw
Linn
(Waterfall)

E

85

Sheepfolds

Highste

The Shanks

Contours are given in metres
The vertical interval is 10m

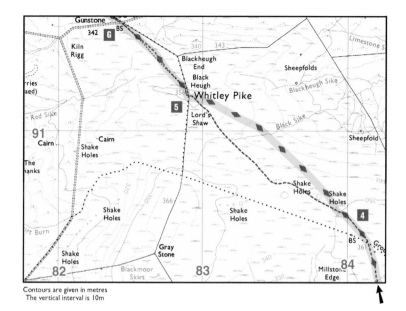

Contours are given in metres
The vertical interval is 10m

The Way forks at a signpost **E**, GPS 53°
53.821 02° 03.573, the official route
making for the higher ground, while an
alternative route keeps to the lower
ground, rejoining the main trail west of
Hareshaw House **1**. On the normal route,
if the path goes missing in action, head
due north to Hareshaw House. Squelch
through a boggy section, cross Hazel Burn
on a footbridge, turn right on to the farm
road and left over a ladder-stile after the
first building. After the farmyard, the Way
takes a wide track **2**, formerly a small
coal-carrying railway line, past a quarry
and workings and out on to the B6320
(west to Bellingham, east to the A68 and
Otterburn).

Cross over, angling right, north-north-
east, past an old mine and its spoil heap
3, GPS 53° 54.536 02° 04.133. The
path can get jumbled here, so look out for
posts ahead. The circular stone enclosure
to the west pre-dates any industrial relics
and is a kind of sheepfold, called a 'stell'.

Head for a post and as the ground rises
steadily there are few other obvious
landmarks except for grouse butts **F**.

Head towards the butts, following the
path through the heather as it bears
north-east then north-west. The hill is
Deer Play **4**, a soggy wilderness with
limitless views. Wainwright though the
next section 'a dreary slog' and 'without
interest'. But it's a delicious portion of
moorland in the September sunshine,
which brings the purple heather to life.
The name hints that perhaps red deer
were once hunted here, but they're long
gone. Roe deer, however, have thrived
because of the forest plantations and can
sometimes be seen, though not usually far
from cover.

The route descends north-west, rising by a
vague path to the cone of Whitley Pike **5**,
GPS 55° 12.906 02° 16.189. From the
summit the route heads north-west,
straight downhill on a stone-slabbed path,
making for a cattle grid and gates over an
unfenced road **G**, GPS 55° 13.165 02°
16.659. Route-finding is easier now, as the
Way follows a fence for several miles and
those wonderful views continue. By now
you should be able to see the Cheviots
again, rising challengingly to the north.

The fence leads north-west towards Padon, past a sandstone boulder **6** and passing the brow of the **Padon Hill 7** to the west. A stile over the fence allows access to the pepper-pot-style cairn, the highest point since Cross Fell, with excellent views over Redesdale and Otterburn to the east, near to where the

Battle of Otterburn was fought in 1388. The Scots, who captured 'Harry Hotspur', beat the English, who killed Earl Douglas of Scotland and the story is told in a ballad popularised by Sir Walter Scott (who also has a poem about High Force).

From Padon Hill the route keeps to the fence, dropping down to a marshy saddle

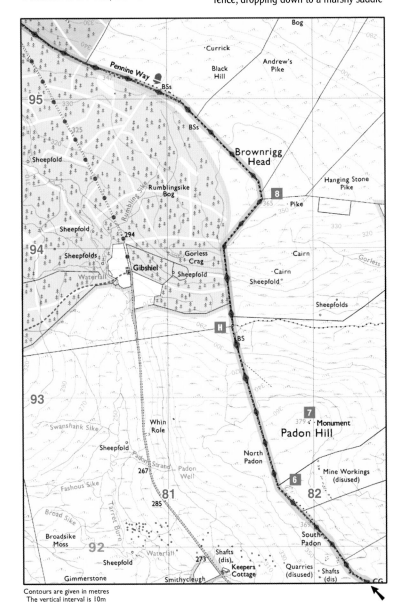

Contours are given in metres
The vertical interval is 10m

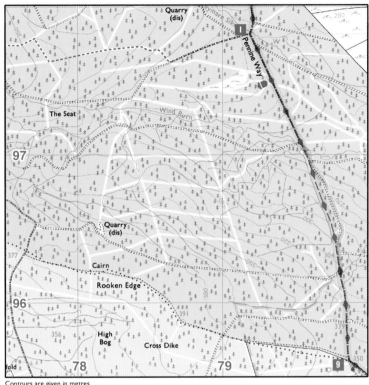

Contours are given in metres
The vertical interval is 10m

, then rising via a stiff if short ascent to Brownrigg Head , GPS 55° 14.572 02° 17.409. From here there are fine views north-east to the Cheviot massif and south to Padon Hill, while ominous plantations of spruce trees begin to darken the landscape to the north-west, including Kielder.

The Way continues along a squelchy stretch for some time, with forest on one side and open moorland on the other. Stones bearing the letters GH show the boundary of the old Redesdale estate of Gabriel Hall, High Sheriff of Northumberland in 1705. Eventually the route arcs westwards and into the trees. I could see another forest within the forest here: red toadstools, which had been merrily munched on during wild feasting by some unidentified creatures (most likely trolls or goblins).

The twilight world of Kielder is entered at Rookengate , GPS 55° 15.187 02°

17.466, where an old sign welcomes Pennine Way walkers. Once through the gate and on the wide forest drive (keep an ear and eye out for forestry vehicles), it's both a relief and a disappointment to find that the forest isn't nearly as claustrophobic as it hinted at being, plus the ground is firm (hoorah!).

Occasional views reveal high hills to the north and moorland to the east, and a constant twittering of birds is mostly coaltits, chaffinches and crossbills. There is a chance of seeing sparrowhawks or goshawks here too – predators who benefit from the seclusion of the forest.

Before the little stone bridge over Greymare Sike , GPS 55° 16.444 02° 19.739, you're invited to leave the track briefly to the right, but you may wish you hadn't bothered. It leaves you battling shoulder-high bracken and is unsteady

Bellingham to Byness

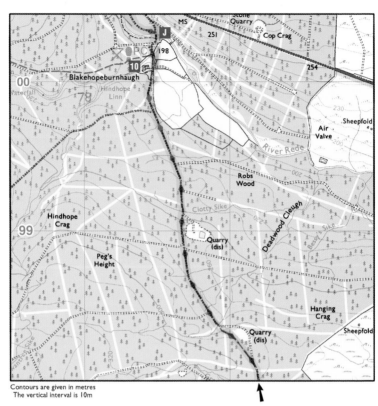

Contours are given in metres
The vertical interval is 10m

underfoot before returning you to the drive a few minutes later with a new appreciation of gravel.

After several miles the drive descends and the green pastures of Redesdale finally appear through the trees, including the farmstead of **Blakehopeburnhaugh 10**. Turn right after a toilet block, take the bridge **J** over the River Rede ('rede' means 'red', a reference to the colour of the water), then turn left. The route keeps to the east bank of the Rede, towards Cottonshopeburnfoot.

Cross a bridge **K** to the west bank and continue along a forest track through a plantation before turning right, downhill **L**, GPS 55° 18.643 02° 21.806, across the Rede again and past a picnic site and the little Holy Trinity Church **11** into Byrness **12**.

If you need to cross the A68, it is fast and furious, so take care. Facilities may be few here, but it's a welcome sight for tired trekkers. Get some rest. The Cheviots beckon.

Public transport

Byrness (on route)

Refreshments, public toilets and information

Byrness (on route) The Byrness,

Forest View

Toilets: Blakehopeburnhaugh

Accommodation

Byrness (on route) The Byrness, Forest View, Forest Caravan Park

Wild roe deer have thrived because of the forest plantations and can sometimes be seen, though not usually far from cover.

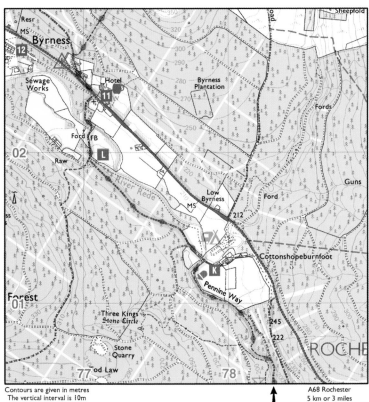

Contours are given in metres
The vertical interval is 10m

A68 Rochester
5 km or 3 miles

15 Byrness to Windy Gyle

past Chew Green and over Beefstand Hill
14 miles (22 km)

Ascent 2,618 feet (798 metres)

Descent 1,591 feet (485 metres)

Highest point Windy Gyle: 2,030 feet (619 metres)

Lowest point Byrness: 755 feet (230 metres)

Around 27 miles (43 km), along the top of the loneliest hills in the least-populated part of England, is all that stands between you and graduation to a Pennine Wayfarer.

As I walked south–north, every time I met a walker coming the other direction I asked them what their favourite bit had been. Several mentioned Middleton-in-Teesdale to Dufton, and Malham got votes. But one guy thought for longer than the others. 'The Cheviots were the best part,' he said assuredly. I agree with him. In a nutshell, today is brilliant; tomorrow is even better.

Route-finding is surprisingly easy. The path often follows the fence that marks the border between England and Scotland – pretty much the only human-made item you'll see. There are bogs, of course, and up here they're of the 'where's my walking pole gone?' variety. It can be exposed, too, and this is also a military training area (blank firing only), so don't touch anything strange, metal or bomb-shaped.

Some nutters attempt to walk to Kirk Yetholm in one madcap dash from here, but it's a shame to be too knackered to take in the wonderful views. Though there are no facilities in the Cheviots, there are several convenient ways of splitting the traverse in two.

For those happy roughing it, two emergency huts are options if you have the right equipment, though they're smaller and more rudimentary than Greg's Hut. The first probably arrives sooner than is ideal, but the second is a manageable night-stop, leaving only about 6.5 miles (10 km) to Kirk Yetholm. Take plenty of drinking water.

There's accommodation in the Coquet Valley if you leave the Way at Plea Knowe and follow The Street downhill – it's about 3.5 miles (5.6 km) to accommodation.

The most popular arrangement is to take advantage of one of the two accommodation providers in Byrness, who will collect you from Trows Farm, Upper Coquette, which is about halfway through the Cheviots, and take you back the next morning. This option involves a 1.5-mile (2.4-km) steep but spectacular descent from the summit of Windy Gyle (and ascent the next morning) and is the version followed in this book. (See page 187 for contact information.) You can also get to the Coquet Valley from Trows Farm. Also, from Clennell Street, a little further on (see page 182), you could descend 2.5 miles (4 km) to Cocklawfoot Farm to be collected (and returned in the morning) by accommodation providers in Kirk Yetholm.

In the College Valley, which arrives after the second hut, there's a youth hostel, about 1.5 miles (2.4 km) off route. In all cases, book ahead to avoid unpleasant surprises.

Things to look out for

◼ **Cheviot Hills** The Cheviots are legendary lumps, and not only for their bogs. They're massive, nay monstrous, round things, shaped like cartoon hills – they're wild, they're windy and they're wonderful. Their geological history is quite different from the Pennines. They were created by the lava from volcanoes 380 million years ago, when it cooled to form andesite – a range of mountains that may have resembled the Andes today (hence the name of the rock). When the volcanoes had stopped, an upwelling of magma beneath the hills left the Cheviots with a core of granite. Because it cooled slowly, deep under ground, this granite is composed of large crystals (unlike volcanic rocks like the dolerite of the Whin Sill) made up of quartz, feldspar and mica. Where the hot granite touched the andesite, it cooked and hardened it. The Cheviots were once an island surrounded by a shallow sea; at another time they were a headland looking out over an immense river. Eventually water worked its way into the massif to create valleys, while glaciers also chipped in to help create the current bulbous landscape.

The Cheviots, and the summit of Windy Gyle in particular, were Tom Stephenson's favourite part of the Way. The two conical summits of The Schil and White Law are almost as good for stupendous views and a sense of glorious loneliness. The Cheviots are a fittingly wonderful finale to the Pennine Way.

◼ **Bombs** The Ministry of Defence owns 20 per cent of Northumberland National Park, which has brought criticism and controversy ever since the Park was created in 1956, and it does put a small dampener on some otherwise wonderful walking. Some training happens here and signs bluntly warn of the dangers: 'Do not touch anything. It may explode and kill you'

(being dead would of course make finishing the Pennine Way rather troublesome). You may also see soldiers about, possibly carrying much heavier packs than yours. Bottomless bogs apart, however, the path itself is safe and no live ammunition is used here.

◼ **Wild things** After being released in College Valley in the mid-19th century, herds of wild goats have survived in the Cheviots. After the October rut they range down into the valleys searching for better grazing. Wild goats come in many shapes and sizes, but are most often grey. The billies are big, long-horned and long-haired. As well as merlins, buzzards and black grouse, golden eagles are occasionally seen around here. Hills often have bird names too, proving their long history with the area: Gowkhope ('gowk' is cuckoo), Cushat Law ('cushat' is woodpigeon), Cocklaw ('cock' is woodcock) and Corbies Crag ('corbie' is carrion crow).

🖽 **Windy Gyle** You'll soon have a good idea of how Windy Gyle, one of the most charismatic of the Cheviot summits (2,030 feet/619 metres), got its name. The mound of stones on the summit is called Russell's Cairn and dates from the Bronze Age. After the Middle Ages the Border region was split into three marches, each ruled by a lord. There were regular meetings between wardens at remote crossing points, but they sometimes degenerated into squabbles and even bloodbaths. The Hanging Stone on the slopes of Cairn Hill was used for such meetings, as was Russell's Cairn, where Lord Francis Russell was murdered at a meeting in 1585. Putting the hill's sinister history aside, the North Sea is sometimes visible from here, amongst a whole lot more, and you can see why Tom Stephenson so enjoyed this place. It's one of the highlights of the Way.

Route description

After crossing the A68 by the Holy Trinity Church in Byrness, head left along it for 50 potentially hairy yards, then up a tarmac path to a gate beside Byrness Cottage . (From Byrness village, a short road walk south-east, crossing to a wide tarmac drive, leads up to the same gate.) From the gate, cross a field, then go through another gate and across a forest drive and uphill on a path through a mixed conifer plantation.

The path is steep and potentially slippy, but if you manage not to fall flat on your face (like one guidebook writer may have done),

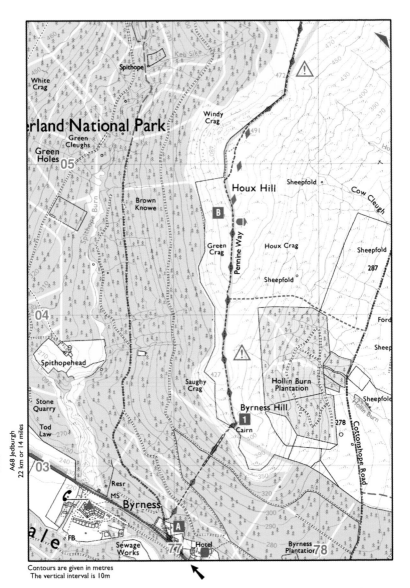

Contours are given in metres
The vertical interval is 10m

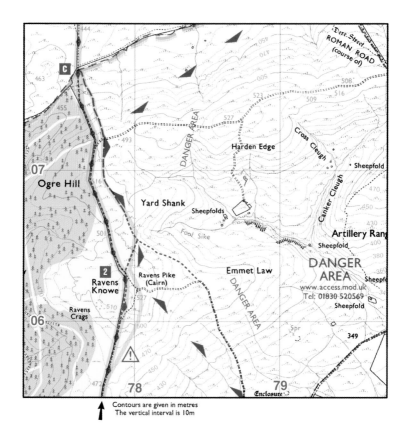

Contours are given in metres
The vertical interval is 10m

its uncompromising line wastes no time in gaining height and leaving the forest behind. After a gate and a short scramble up a rock edge, you reach the brow of Byrness Hill and the remains of a stone fire-lookout tower and a hexagonal hut **1**.

You are at the threshold of a different world. To the north is an open ridge, often pummelled by wind and rain. If the weather's good, it's glorious. If it's not, the going can be – what's a nice word for it? – testing. Good luck.

The Way heads north-west, along the broad crest of the ridge, past an MOD sign and Saughy Crag head, to Houx Hill **B**, which has no summit marker, so in rough weather aim for a post just after it, GPS 55° 18.917 02° 21.713, and follow the fence.

Your feet are probably about to revert back to their familiar state of sogginess in the day's first batch of bogs. These are the type of bog that, when you insert your walking pole to gauge the depth, it carries on downwards unchecked.

The Way keeps to the high ground, to Ravens Knowe **2**, GPS 55° 20.968 02° 20.895, which has excellent views, then continues over duckboards to Ogre Hill. Though the map shows trees to the west, they've recently been cut down. Descend over boggy ground to the Border fence and through a gate **C**, GPS 55° 21.754 02° 21.296, into Scotland. (The exact line of the Border is arbitrary, depending on where each generation of farmers put the fence.)

The path leads north for a few hundred yards, then forks right , GPS 55° 21.941 02°21.143, and drops down. The route takes you around Chew Green , a green maze of earthworks that were once a Roman marching camp designed for an assault on the Scots by Agricola and his Ninth Army.

The Pennine Way leads east, then bears north-west around the edge of the earthworks. At , GPS 55° 22.137 02° 19.787, turn left, north, and uphill. Halfway up the hill the Way bears right, north-east, over a bridge , GPS 55° 22.353 02° 20.229, to pick up the ancient trackway Dere Street , a Roman road that once linked York with Scotland. Follow this to the Border fence to the north-east of Brownhart Law, close to a Roman signal station .

The Way heads northwards along the Border Ridge, but at a five-bar gate , GPS 55° 23.330 02° 20.113, Dere Street braches off left and the Way stays on the high ridge making for a mound with a peat-built cairn and a post . A clear path then leads north, away from the Border fence, arcing eastwards via stone cairns and posts, and across marshy ground with short boardwalks over sikes and burns.

The Way crosses more boggy ground at the head of Rennies Burn , with the fleeting help of a wooden bridge, GPS 55° 23.871 02° 20.171, where there are some basins of Molinia grass .

A welcome wooden bridge at the head of Rennes Burn, where you'll probably see big clumps of Molinia grass.

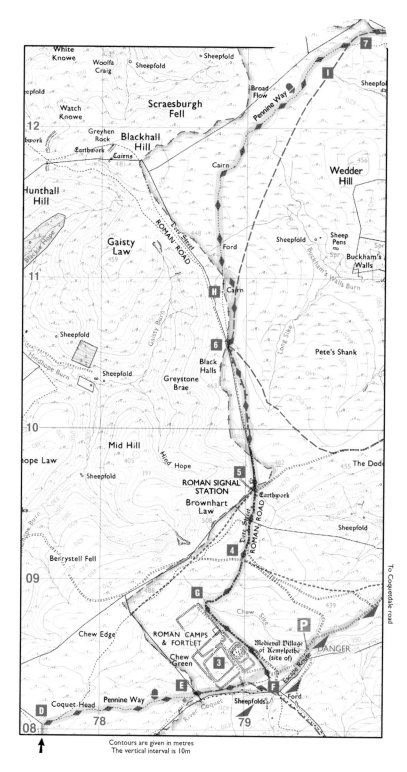

Contours are given in metres
The vertical interval is 10m

Back along the Border fence, now heading east, expansive views start opening up (weather permitting, as always). The Scottish side opens its kilt to reveal the verdant lowlands of the Teviot Valley and Tweedsdale, the Eildon Hills by Melrose, and in the far distance the Lammermuir and Moorfoot Hills stand in front of Edinburgh.

The Way turns sharp left **J** at a fence corner, heading north-north-east, and drops down to a gap in the Border Ridge called Yearning Saddle. Here there's a wooden hut **8**, GPS 55° 23.873 02° 20.171, maintained by the National Park Authority for walkers. It's massively welcome to anyone who's endured the worst of the Cheviot's weather. Inside, a clothes line and pegs show what the hut's usually used for.

I arrived here soaked through, wind-battered and feeling a tiny bit sorry for myself . . . only to discover the friendly face of a Bristolian bloke I'd been walking with a few days previously, drying off after a misadventure with a bog. Thirty minutes later the surly clouds were replaced with glorious sunshine and the next stretch had some of the best views – and weather – of the entire walk. A microcosm of the traumas and triumphs of the Pennine Way – as is the hut's visitors' book.

From the Yearning Saddle hut and its view of The Kip **9** to the left, the Way follows the Border fence for several miles, only leaving it to cut obvious corners, and this is where the Cheviots start to get special.

The ridge links a chain of high hills, including Lamb Hill, which has magical views looking back, Beefstand and Mozie Law. From Beefstand **10**, too, there's a classic view right into the cold granite

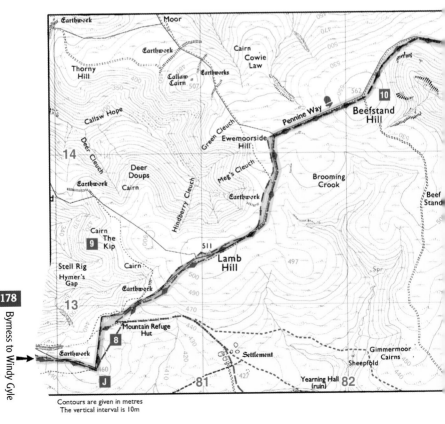

Contours are given in metres
The vertical interval is 10m

heart of the Cheviots: the wide whaleback of The Cheviot itself, with its henchmen, Hedgehope and The Schil.

After the summit of Mozie Law 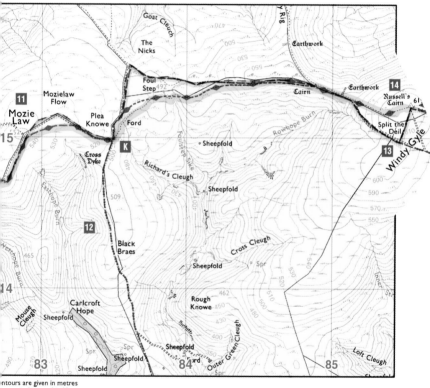11, GPS 55°25.717 02°16.233, the route cuts off a fence corner before Plea Knowe K, then leaves the fence again to avoid a marshy patch aptly called Foul Step.

The track along the crest of the ridge is The Street 12, an ancient drove road, and ahead is **Windy Gyle** 13. The ascent is direct, a stile providing access to the summit, which is on the Scottish side. The mound of stones, GPS 55° 23.802 02° 13.439, is Russell's Cairn 14, which marks a special spot. It's also the logical halfway point of the Cheviot traverse and some will detour from here, heading down to the Coquet Valley, approximately south, for a lift back to Byrness for the night.

ntours are given in metres
he vertical interval is 10m

Public transport

None

Refreshments

Coquet Valley (3.5 miles/5.6 km)
🐦 Barrowburn

Accommodation

Coquet Valley (3.5 miles/5.6 km)
Barrowburn

Kirk Yetholm (but will collect from Cocklawfoot Farm) The Singing Donkeys Hostel

College Valley (1.5 miles/2.4 km) Mount Hooley YHA Bunkhouse

16 Windy Gyle to Kirk Yetholm

past The Cheviot and over The Schil
13 miles (21 km)

Ascent 2,411 feet (735 metres)
Descent 3,838 feet (1,170 metres)
Highest point The Cheviot: 2,674 feet (815 metres)
Lowest point Kirk Yetholm: 382 feet (116 metres)

All that stands between you and Pennine Way immortality is... a lot more big hills, some very strong winds and a few hungry bogs.

Today is very much like yesterday, only marginally superior for scenery, less boggy and with a spectacular, long and possibly quite emotional descent at the end. In fair weather, it's the sort of day you wish would go on for ever. But sadly your walk is nearly at its end. You've got some choices to make: firstly, whether to detour to the top of The Cheviot and back, and secondly whether to take the higher or lower routes for the final descent.

There are no services along the way and route-finding is easier than yesterday. So make the most of it.

Finishing the Pennine Way should be a triumphant and deeply satisfying experience. But don't expect cheering crowds and autograph-hunters in Kirk Yetholm. The good people of this tiny Border town see Wayfarers finish all the time. Nevertheless, you have done great things. You know it and I know it.

Things to look out for

■ **Border badlands** The Cheviot wilderness was a place for outlaws. Much of the area between the Border Gate and King's Seat was once wooded, but outrageously cheeky Scottish raiders of the 14th and 15th centuries have been blamed for stealing, bit by bit, a whole forest. Highlander Black Rory ran several illicit stills here, too; one was at the foot of Davidson's Burn, to the south-east of King's Seat.

Hanging Stone marked the boundary between the Middle March and East March in the days when the Borderlands were governed by marcher lords. You're probably not very interested, but the Halls may be originally from these parts, and my dad, a keen horseman, likes to think we were very much part of the Border, er, lifestyle. If true, I'm proud to be associated with reiver or outlaw stock – die on your feet rather than live on your knees and all that. I like to think we were a bit mischievous, stole the odd horse – you know, mostly from the rich – but were essentially good folk. Though, some cursory research indicates we were possibly more on the treacherous side of things. So, um, let's leave it at that, eh, and get on with some quality walking.

■ Iron Age forts The Cheviots were once alive with the sounds of hills forts. Between White Law and Yeavering Bell (off route, but visible) lies Great Hetha, an Iron Age fort. The twin-peaked summit of the Bell is likewise encircled by a stone rampart and the traces of 130 Iron Age houses. Meanwhile, the Anglo-Saxon palace of Ad Gefrin, where the kings of Northumbria Aethelfrith and Edwin held court, lies below Yeavering Bell. In fact, most suitable hills around here had settlements of some kind and the population was considerably greater 2,000 years ago than it is now.

2 The Cheviot The Cheviot stands entirely in England, 'because the Scots wanted no part of it,' said Wainwright. This is the ugly great lump of a hill that's been taunting you for the last few days and comparisons with Jabba the Hutt don't feel entirely wide of the mark. At 2,674 feet (815 metres) it's a lofty summit, the highest in Northumberland and the second-highest place on the Way after the Cross Fell–Great Dun Fell range. Although, because it is such a broad whaleback, the views from the top are disappointing.

It's not strictly on the route, but the detour isn't far and the path is stone-flagged all the way. The summit is a desolate, apocalyptical place, unfriendly and wind-battered. But it feels good to trample over The Cheviot's big, ugly, bullying head (yes, it got personal).

In December 1944 a Flying Fortress (US bomber) crashed here during an afternoon blizzard. Two shepherds received the British Empire Medal for helping to save seven of the crew (two died), while their dog was awarded the Dickin Medal, the animal's Victoria Cross.

11 Kirk Yetholm Once a gypsy settlement, Kirk Yetholm is a name that's probably been on your lips for weeks now. Way rumours paint it as some sort of ghost town in the middle of nowhere. It is small, transport links aren't exhaustive and if you try to get away on a Sunday you're in for some fun, but Kirk Yetholm is a comely, friendly little place. And it has around seven buses to Kelso every weekday (plus taxis are another option). The Border Hotel, or the bus stop, is the traditional Pennine Way finishing point. The Border Hotel will issue you a certificate and offer you a Wayfarers' book to sign, which includes comments like, 'We carried sunscreen for 280 miles!' And 'Started as a school girl. Finished as an OAP' (they must have got pretty badly lost). Better still, you're entitled to a free half pint. Alfred Wainwright used to pay the bill, which reached £15,000. The pub continues the reward scheme, but only if you did the walk in one go. 'How do you know claimants are genuine?' I asked the barman, feeling I already knew the answer. 'Oh, you can tell,' he said.

The views from Auchope Cairn towards The Schil are pretty special, but it's usually very, very windy.

Route description

From the summit of Windy Gyle the Way leads north-east along the fence-line (the English side has flagstones) to descend sharply before levelling off. Go past the amusingly named Blair's Hole (you can't see it, but it seems worth a mention) and after 0.5 mile (1 km) an old drove road cuts across the ridge at a ladder-stile and gate **A**, GPS 55° 26.078 02° 12.958. This is Clennell Street, once the busiest of all the ancient Border crossings and used by drovers, soldiers and reivers. It can be followed north-west down to Cocklawfoot (an overnight option).

The Way sticks to the fence, which seems inappropriate for an international frontier, but there is little stone for a wall, let alone a building for passport inspection.

The Way leads north-north-east past the King's Seat triangulation point **B**, GPS 55° 26.988 02° 11.578, then turns north-east with the fence up to Cairn Hill. The ascent is steep, but there are flags then duckboards. Ahead is the great dome of The Cheviot and the little outcrop of rocks on the brow of the hill to the right, which looks like a couple of fangs, is the Hanging Stone **1**. Bilberry, cowberry and crowberry, plus cloudberry, a dwarf relative of the raspberry all grow here.

The top of the hill is a quagmire and the boardwalk leads to a junction of fences **C**, GPS 55° 28.082 02° 09.979. The Pennine Way heads left, while right leads to the top **The Cheviot 2**. If there are no scallywags, reivers or backpack-hustlers around, you could leave your bag at the

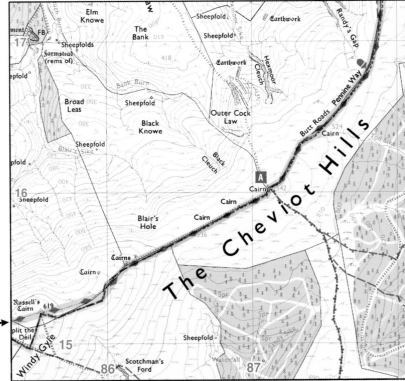

Contours are given in metres
The vertical interval is 10m

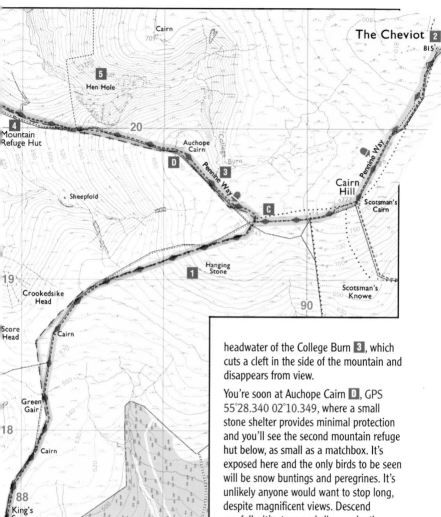

The Cheviot **2** 815

5 Hen Hole

4 Mountain Refuge Hut

20

Auchope Cairn

Pennine Way

Cairn 709

Sheepfold

D

3

Cairn Hill 777

Scotsman's Cairn

C

19

Hanging Stone

1

Crookedsike Head

Scotsman's Knowe

90

Score Head

Cairn

Green Gair

18

Cairn

88

King's Seat 531 **B**

89

Contours are given in metres
The vertical interval is 10m

gate. It's possible to be back in about 30 minutes, sans pack.

The Way heads left, north-west, at the stile, crossing another quagmire of liquid peat via duckboards (if you can get to the end without getting a walking pole stuck between planks - I couldn't - reward yourself with chocolate or an equivalent confectionary treat). To the right is the

headwater of the College Burn **3**, which cuts a cleft in the side of the mountain and disappears from view.

You're soon at Auchope Cairn **D**, GPS 55°28.340 02°10.349, where a small stone shelter provides minimal protection and you'll see the second mountain refuge hut below, as small as a matchbox. It's exposed here and the only birds to be seen will be snow buntings and peregrines. It's unlikely anyone would want to stop long, despite magnificent views. Descend carefully, it's steep and slippery, by the north-west path and make for the hut **4**, GPS 55° 28.508 02° 11.764. As ever, reading and signing the visitors' book is an essential part of Pennine Way culture.

From here the Way follows a clear path, still parallel with the Border fence, along a ridge. The views are glorious; west to former lover Windy Gyle, and east to the Hen Hole **5**, a hanging valley formed by retreating glaciers 10,000 years ago – the highlight of the day, thought Wainwright, oddly. To the north is College Valley,

Windy Gyle to Kirk Yetholm

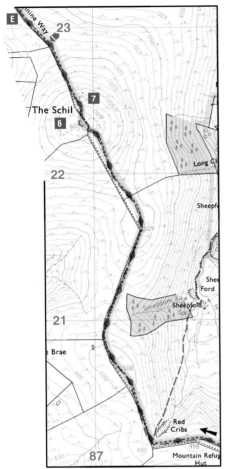

Contours are given in metres
The vertical interval is 10m

The sweep downhill still sticks with the Border and leads to a ladder-stile and signpost **E**, GPS 55° 30.198 02° 13.045, in the wall on a saddle between The Schil and Black Hag, telling you it's just 4.75 miles (7.6 km) to the Pennine Way's end (Yay! Noo!). Next there's a ladder-stile **F** over the wall to the left.

The Way crosses it into Scotland and you'll not set foot in England again on the walk. A path leads north-west, below Corbie Craig and above the head of the Rowhope Burn, but after only a few hundred yards the Way forks **G**, GPS 55° 30.312 02° 13.454, offering a choice between high- and low-level routes.

If you just want to get it all over with, take the left fork for the low-level route, to be in Kirk Yetholm in about 1.5 hours. This becomes a track, then follows a path north along the Halter Burn, providing an easy and pleasant descent into Kirk Yetholm. However, the high-level route may be 30 minutes longer, but it keeps with the Border Ridge to the very end, extracting the last drop of exhilaration from this great walk. Well worth it, if you've got the energy. Going down in a blaze of glory and all that.

On the high-level route, after Steerrig Knowe **H**, GPS 55° 30.593 02° 13.743, the Way heads north-north-east through a gate, keeping to the grassy ridge of Steer Rig, losing height all the time. Ahead is the twin-cairned summit of Coldsmouth Hill. To the west are the Cheviot foothills and the green fields of the Bowmont. To the east is the treeless valley of the Trowup Burn **8** with the hills rising from it dappled like horses.

The terrain is grassy and firm and the last testing climb lies ahead as the Way turns north-west to White Law **9**. The slopes are steep, but the summit yields yet more wondrous views: north-west to the Lammermuir Hills, east to the outer Cheviots, above the mouth of the College and Yeavering Bell, the most important archaeological site in the region.

reputedly named after a coven of witches, and some way beyond lie the coastal plain and the North Sea.

The Schil **6**, GPS 55° 29.682 02° 12.471, is the last big hill on the route and perhaps the finest of all. Wainwright thought so. The climb up is short and sharp and the charismatic yet cynical old crags on the top provide a stirring panoramic setting. Descending on the north side, there are several outcrops **7**, remnants of a metamorphic aureole. The views, as ever, are spectacular, though don't bother trying to locate that pesky Kirk Yetholm – it's tucked out of view, still hiding from you.

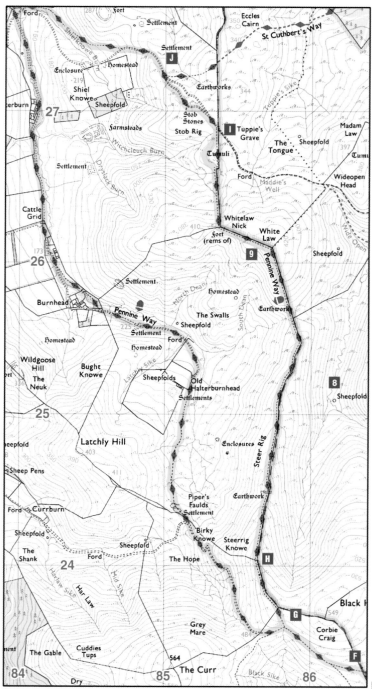

Contours are given in metres
The vertical interval is 10m

The Way begins its final, emotional, descent to the Bowmont Valley and you may find yourself in two minds. I wanted to get back to my wife and baby daughter after a long time away (will the little lady still recognise me? Heck, will my wife still recognise me?). But I realised I was walking slower than usual, savouring the last moments: the views, the physical sensations – even the wind, that long-term foe, began to feel like a familiar friend.

Cross a ladder-stile 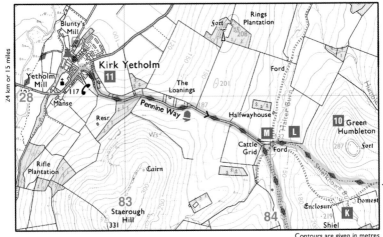, GPS 55° 31.774 02° 13.993, and head downhill, beside a wall, until a track goes obliquely left, GPS 55° 32.135 02° 14.025, signed at the wall, where the Way drops down along a green track. Green Humbleton, up ahead, is a grassy hill crowned by an Iron Age hill fort. But the Way is finally in uncharacteristically charitable mood and lets you angle left around its lower slopes. Ignore a left, then follow the Shielknowe Burn down to meet the Halter Burn.

The Way meets a tarmac road at a cattle grid, GPS 55° 32.547 02° 15.349, and bears right to follow this west-north-west for the last mile of the journey, starting with an unfair little ascent. Did you really expect the Pennine Way to let you go without a fight? It's the very last one.

It's important to enjoy times like these, the last sad but glorious moments of freedom. But questions will inevitably arise. Has the Pennine Way changed you? Is there another walk that can match this one for scenery, drama and a sense of achievement? (Some give up looking and just do the Pennine Way again.) Will you ever be able to wash the peat out from under your toenails?

The houses of Kirk Yetholm soon signal the finishing line and a return to the world of dry feet. Congratulations, lonesome bog-trotter, you've just walked the Pennine Way. You should feel very proud. Wasn't it something, eh?

Public transport
Kirk Yetholm (on route)

Refreshments
Kirk Yetholm (on route) Border Hotel
Town Yetholm (1 mile/1.6 km) Plough
Food shops: Town Yetholm (1 mile/1.6 km)

Accommodation
Kirk Yetholm (on route) wide selection
Town Yetholm (1 mile/1.6 km) Plough Hotel

Contours are given in metres
The vertical interval is 10m

Useful Information

This list includes details of websites, email addresses and telephone numbers, where available. If no email address is shown, it may be possible to send an email via the website. Pennine Way National Trail Office www.nationaltrail.co.ukpennineway.

National Trails Office
ⓘ www.nationaltrail.co.uk

Transport
Megabus
ⓘ www.uk.megabus.com
☎ 0900 1600900

National Rail Enquiries
ⓘ www.nationalrail.co.uk
☎ 08457 48 49 50

National Express
ⓘ www.nationalexpress.co.uk
☎ 08717 818178

Taxi Service for Kirk Yetholm
☎ 01835 863755/01835 863039

Transport Direct
ⓘ www.transportdirect.info

Traveline
ⓘ www.traveline.org.uk
☎ 0871 2002233

Accommodation
The Pennine Way Association
ⓘ www.penninewayassociation.co.uk/accommodation

Pennine Way National Trail
ⓘ www.nationaltrail.co.uk/pennineway

The Byrness
ⓘ www.thebyrness.co.uk
☎ 01830 520231

Forest View
ⓘ www.forestviewbyrness.co.uk
☎ 07928 376677 / 01830 520425

Tan Hill Inn
ⓘ www.tanhillinn.co.uk
☎ 01833 628 246

Youth Hostel Association
ⓘ www.yha.org.uk

Baggage-forwarding, accommodation-booking and guiding companies
Brigantes
ⓘ www.brigantesenglishwalks.com

Discovery Travel
ⓘ www.discoverytravel.co.uk

Macs Adventure
ⓘ www.macsadventure.com

The Sherpa Van Project
ⓘ www.sherpavan.com

UK Exploratory
ⓘ www.alpineexploratory.com/ukexploratory.html

Tourist information
Alston Tourist Information Centre
☎ 01434 382244

Bellingham Tourist Information Centre
☎ 01434 220616

Edale Visitor Centre
☎ 01433 670207

Hawes National Park Centre
✉ hawes@yorkshiredales.org.uk
☎ 01969 666210

Haworth Visitor Information Centre
✉ haworth@ytbtic.co.uk
☎ 01535 642329

Hebden Bridge Tourist Information
ⓘ www.hebdenbridge.co.uk
☎ 01422 843831

Horton in Ribblesdale Information (Pen-y-ghent Café)
☎ 01729 860333

Marsden Tourist Information Centre
✉ marsden.visitorinformation@kirklees.gov.uk
☎ 01484 222555

Middleton-in-Teesdale Information
☎ 01833 641001

Northumberland National Park Visitor Centre
☎ 01434 344396

Peak District Tourist Information
- www.visitpeakdistrict.com

Todmorden Tourist Information Centre
- www.visittodmorden.co.uk
- ☎ 01706 818181

Yorkshire Dales National Park Centre (Malham)
- ☎ 01729 833200

Other contacts

Backpackers Club
- www.backpackersclub.co.uk
- ☎ inforequest@backpackersclub.co.uk

Boots and Paws
- www.bootsandpaws.co.uk
- ✉ mail@bootsandpaws.co.uk

Bowes Museum
- www.bowesmuseum.org.uk
- ☎ 01833 690606

Bowes Railway
- www.bowesrailway.co.uk
- ☎ 0191 4161847

Brontë Parsonage Museum
- www.bronte.org.uk
- ☎ 01535 642323

Dales Countryside Museum
- www.yorkshiredales.org.uk/dcm
- ☎ 01969 666210

English Heritage
- www.english-heritage.org.uk
- ☎ 08703 331181

Friends of the Settle–Carlisle Line (FofSCL)
- www.foscl.org.uk

Live for the Outdoors
- www.livefortheoutdoors.com

Long Distance Walkers Association
- www.ldwa.org.uk

National Trust
- www.nationaltrust.org.uk
- ☎ 0844 800 1895

Natural England
- www.naturalengland.org.uk
- ✉ enquiries@naturalengland.org.uk
- ☎ 0845 6003078

North Pennines Area of Outstanding Natural Beauty
- www.northpennines.org.uk
- ☎ 01388 528801

Northumberland National Park
- www.northumberlandnationalpark.org.uk
- ☎ 01434 605555

Ordnance Survey
- www.ordnancesurvey.co.uk
- ☎ 08456 050505

Peak District National Park Authority
- www.peakdistrict.gov.uk
- ☎ 01629 816200

Pennine Bridleway National Trail
- www.nationaltrail.co.uk/penninebridleway

Pennine Way Association
- www.penninewayassociation.co.uk
- ✉ penninewayassociation@hotmail.com

Ramblers
- www.ramblers.org.uk
- ☎ 020 7339 8500

Ropemakers (Hawes)
- www.ropemakers.co.uk
- ☎ 01969 667487

Royal Society for the Protection of Birds (RSPB)
- www.rspb.org.uk
- ☎ 01767 680551

Standedge Tunnel Visitor Centre
- www.standedge.co.uk
- ☎ 01484 847810

Wainwright Society
- www.wainwright.org.uk
- ✉ webmaster@wainwright.org.uk

Walking on the Web
- www.walkingontheweb.co.uk
- ☎ 01347 868382

Wensleydale Creamery
- www.wensleydale.co.uk
- ☎ 01969 667664

Wildlife Trusts
- www.wildlifetrusts.org
- ☎ 01636 677711

Yorkshire Dales National Park
- www.yorkshiredales.org.uk
- ☎ 0300 456 0030

Bibliography

Bibby, Andrew, *The Backbone of England: Landscape and Life on the Pennine Watershed* (Frances Lincoln, 2008).

Brontë, Emily, *Wuthering Heights* (Penguin, 1847; many editions available).

Burton, Anthony, *Hadrian's Wall Path*, Official National Trail Guide (Aurum Press, 2010).

Davies, Hunter, *Wainwright: the Biography* (Orion, 1995).

Hardy, Graeme, *North to South Along the Pennine Way* (Warne Gerrard, 1983).

Hopkins, Tony, *Northumberland National Park Guide* (Pevensey, 2002).

Hopkins, Tony, *The Cheviot Hills* (Halsgrove, 2003).

Mitchell, W. R., *Hannah Hauxwell: 80 Years in the Dales* (Great Northern Books, 2008).

Oldham, Kenneth, *The Pennine Way* (Dalesman, 1960).

Pilton, Barry, *One Man and His Bog* (Corgi, 1986).

Pitt, David, *A Pennine Journey: From Settle to Hadrian's Wall in Wainwright's Footsteps* (Frances Lincoln, 2010).

Smith, Roly, *The Pennine Way* (Francis Lincoln, 2011).

Stephenson, Tom, *The Pennine Way* (HMSO, 1973).

Wainwright, Alfred, *A Pennine Journey: The Story of a Long Walk in 1938* (Michael Joseph, 1986).

Wainwright, Alfred, *Pennine Way Companion: a Pictorial Guide* (Frances Lincoln, 1968).

Wainwright, Alfred, *Wainwright on the Pennine Way* (Mermaid Books, 1986).

Wallington, Mark, *Pennine Walkies* (Arrow Books, 1997).

Wood, John, *Mountain Trail: the Pennine Way from Peak to Cheviot* (Blackfriars, 1947).

Wright, Christopher John, *A Guide to the Pennine Way* (Constable, 1967).

Pennine Walkies and *One Man and His Bog* are particularly entertaining. Some may find it worth having a Google around for Wayfarers' online diaries too. *The Pennine Way: Great Walks from the Air* (Beckmann, 2006) is a DVD that gives an aerial view of the route. Better still, look on YouTube for Daniel Staniforth's wonderful *Hiking England* video diaries of the Pennine Way from Edale to Bowes (the worse the weather, the happier he seems).

Maps

Landranger (1:50,000) 74, 75, 80, 91, 92, 98, 103, 109, 110

Explorer (1:25,000) OL1 The Peak District (Dark Peak Area); OL2 Yorkshire Dales; OL21 South Pennines; OL21 Yorkshire Dales (Northern and Central Areas); OL16 The Cheviot Hills; OL19 Howgill Fells and Upper Eden Valley; OL31 North Pennines, Teesdale and Weardale; OL42 Kielder Water and Forest; OL43 Hadrian's Wall

Footprint Maps
ⓘ www.footprintmaps.co.uk
Harvey Maps
ⓘ www.harveymaps.co.uk
Memory Map
ⓘ www.memory-map.co.uk

Useful Information

The Official Guides to all of

Cotswold Way
Anthony Burton

100 miles of quintessentially
English landscape

ISBN 978 1 84513 785 4

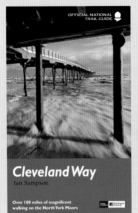

Cleveland Way
Ian Sampson

Over 100 miles of magnificent
walking on the North York Moors

ISBN 978 1 84513 781 6

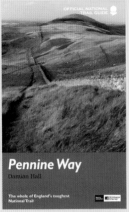

Pennine Way
Damian Hall

The whole of England's toughest
National Trail

ISBN 978 1 84513 718 2

Yorkshire Wolds Way
Roger Ratcliffe

A superbly tranquil walk through the
unspoilt chalk hills of East Yorkshire

ISBN 978 1 84513 643 7

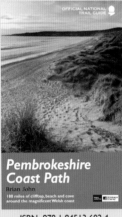

Pembrokeshire
Coast Path
Brian John

180 miles of clifftop, beach and cove
around the magnificent Welsh coast

ISBN 978 1 84513 602 4

South Downs Way
Paul Millmore

100 miles of glorious chalk downland
for the walker, cyclist and horse rider

ISBN 978 1 84513 565 2

Hadrian's Wall Path
Anthony Burton

Follow the Roman Wall
from coast to coast

ISBN 978 1 84513 567 6

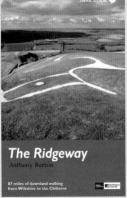

The Ridgeway
Anthony Burton

87 miles of downland walking
from Wiltshire to the Chilterns

ISBN 978 1 84513 638 3

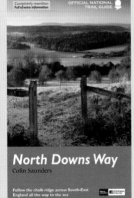

North Downs Way
Colin Saunders

Follow the chalk ridge across South-East
England all the way to the sea

ISBN 978 1 84513 677 2

Britain's National Trails

Thames Path
in the Country
David Sharp and Tony Gowers
From the source to Hampton Court

ISBN 978 1 84513 717 5

Thames Path
in London
Phoebe Clapham
From Hampton Court to Crayford Ness:
50 miles of historic riverside walk

ISBN 978 1 84513 706 9

Peddars Way and
Norfolk Coast Path
Bruce Robinson with Mike Robinson
90 miles from Breckland to
salt marsh and sea cliffs

ISBN 978 1 84513 784 7

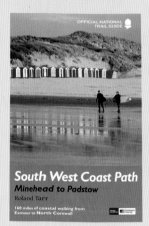

South West Coast Path
Minehead to Padstow
Roland Tarr
160 miles of coastal walking from
Exmoor to North Cornwall

ISBN 978 1 84513 640 6

South West Coast Path
Padstow to Falmouth
John Macadam
From golden beaches to rugged coves
around Britain's southernmost tip

ISBN 978 1 84513 641 3

Offa's Dyke Path
SOUTH: Chepstow to Knighton
Ernie and Kathy Kay and Mark Richards
Follow the ancient earthwork up the Wye
Valley and alongside the Black Mountains

ISBN 978 1 84513 561 4

South West Coast Path
Falmouth to Exmouth
Brian Le Messurier
172 miles of dramatic coves, cliffs and
beaches from Cornwall to Devon

ISBN 978 1 84513 564 5

South West Coast Path
Exmouth to Poole
Roland Tarr
From Jane Austen's Cobb to Lulworth Cove
– over 100 miles of historic coastline

ISBN 978 1 84513 642 0

NATIONAL TRAIL GUIDES
OFFA'S DYKE PATH NORTH
Knighton to Prestatyn
Ernie and Kathy Kay and Mark Richards

100 miles of walking through the
beautiful Welsh marches

ISBN 978 1 84513 312 2

PENNINE BRIDLEWAY
*Derbyshire to the
South Pennines*
Sue Viccars

ISBN 1 85410 957 X

Definitive guides to other popular long-distance walks published by

Camino de Santiago

Sergi Ramis

The ancient Way of Saint James pilgrimage route from the French Pyrenees to Santiago de Compostela

ISBN 978 1 84513 708 3

The Capital Ring

Colin Saunders

78 miles of green corridor encircling inner London

ISBN 978 1 84513 786 1

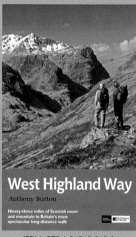

West Highland Way

Anthony Burton

Ninety-three miles of Scottish moor and mountain in Britain's most spectacular long-distance walk

ISBN 978 1 84513 569 0

The London Loop

David Sharp

The walker's M25 – over 140 miles of footpaths in London's secret countryside

ISBN 978 1 84513 787 8

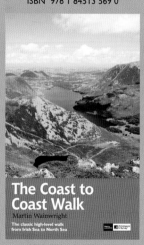

The Coast to Coast Walk

Martin Wainwright

The classic high-level walk from Irish Sea to North Sea

ISBN 978 1 84513 560 7